General Leathercraft

GENERAL LEATHERCRAFT

RAYMOND CHERRY, HEAD

INDUSTRIAL ARTS DEPARTMENT

LOCKPORT TOWNSHIP HIGH SCHOOL

LOCKPORT, ILLINOIS

McKNIGHT & McKNIGHT
PUBLISHING COMPANY
Bloomington, Illinois

Preface to the fourth edition

The many changes in this edition were made to meet the needs of both the homecraftsman and the student interested in all phases of leathercraft. This book was written to be used as a guide and as a source of information so that the reader may develop a worthwhile hobby in leathercraft.

There are many different ways to work leather and to decorate its surfaces. This book will instruct you in many of the old methods and also introduce you to some new ones. All instructional material found in the fundamental operations and the projects has been tested by leathercraft classes or by the homecraftsman.

The "how-to-do" instruction has proved to be sound. A beginner should follow the step-by-step procedures for best results. The teacher of leathercraft will find this book a valuable aid, since the student can readily follow the brief written instructions along with the many photographs of various procedures. This will give the teacher more time to give the needed individual instruction.

The projects and decorative designs are only suggestive. The homecraftsman and the student are always encouraged to design their own projects after they have followed the step-by-step procedure in making some of the projects in this book. Much pride and satisfaction is felt if one does design his own projects.

The tool and supply lists will aid both the beginner and the teacher in ordering from leathercraft supply companies.

A selected book list is given for those who desire to expand their interest and pleasure in working with leather.

Acknowledgments

I wish to acknowledge the help which has been given to me in preparing this book: to my wife credit for typing, checking the manuscript, and helping with the photography; to Ken Griffin for the carvings and carving designs; to Dick Boyt for some of the designs; to the Ohio Leather Company for the material on the manufacture of leather; to the Fiebing Chemical Company for the material on leather finishes; to the C. S. Osborne Company for tools; to many former students and teachers; and to a large number of leathercraft supply companies for their constructive criticisms and for their loyal support of *General Leathercraft* during the past fourteen years.

RAYMOND CHERRY

Table of contents

TOOLS
AND SUPPLIES

The cost of tools and supplies for leathercraft
is very little compared to the value
of the finished articles
which can be produced.
Very few tools need be purchased
to start in leathercraft
either as a hobby or for classwork.
This section describes many
important tools and craft leathers.
The information on dyes, finishes, and dressings
will be very helpful in selecting leather finishes.
The suggested minimum tool list
and recommended additional tool list
and supply check list
for a class of twenty students
will aid teachers in preparing their requisitions.
These lists are found on pages 140 and 141.
The catalogs from leathercraft supply companies
will aid in making the selection
of tools, leather, and other supplies.
Check your local classified telephone directory
for companies in your area.

Tools

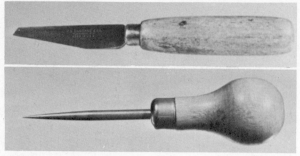

Fig. 1. Bevel point knife — used for cutting leather and for skiving.

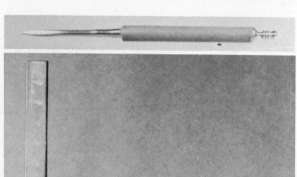

Fig. 2. Scratch awl — used for laying out, opening thong slits, and piercing lightweight leather.

Fig. 3. Tracer — used for tracing designs upon leather and for fine stippling.

Fig. 4. Square — used for measuring and as a guide in cutting leather.

Fig. 5. Modeler — small end is used for tracing designs, tooling, and stippling; flattened end used for modeling.

Fig. 6. Deerfoot modeler — used for putting down backgrounds, beveling, depressing outlines, and getting into small places.

Fig. 7. Ball-end modeler — used for embossing and stippling.

Fig. 8. One-prong thonging chisel — used to make slits for lacing at corners. Two sizes, 3/32" and 1/8".

Fig. 9. Four-prong thonging chisel — used to make equally spaced slits for lacing. Two sizes 3/32" and 1/8".

Fig. 10. Revolving punch — used for punching round holes. Equipped with six tubes of different sizes.

Fig. 11. Round drive punch — used to punch holes where revolving punch cannot be used. Available in several sizes.

Fig. 12. Snap button fastener — used to set birdcage snaps.

Fig. 13. Eyelet setter — used to set eyelets.

Fig. 14. Edge beveler — used to bevel the edges of lightweight leather.

Fig. 15. Common edger — used to round off edges of heavy leather. Available in several sizes.

Fig. 16. Edge creaser — used to crease edges of leather. Available in several sizes.

Fig. 17. Mallet — used for striking stamps, eyelet setter, etc. Made from wood, rawhide, or fiber.

Fig. 18. Stippler — used for rapid stippling of backgrounds.

Fig. 19. Lacing needle — used to lead the lace through thong slits. Has two prongs to keep lace from turning. Other styles available.

Fig. 20. Embossing wheel and carriage — used for border designs. Has interchangeable wheels.

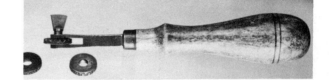

Fig. 21. Space marker — used for marking spaces in hand stitching. Available in several sizes.

Fig. 22. Stitching punch — used to punch uniformly spaced holes for hand stitching in lightweight leather.

Fig. 23. Fid — used for enlarging holes, stippling, and tightening lace.

Fig. 24. Draw gauge — used for cutting heavy leather straps. Adjustable.

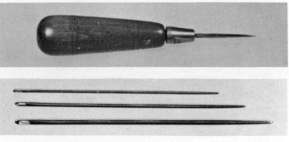

Fig. 25. Saddler's haft and awl — used to make holes for hand sewing. Awls available in several sizes.

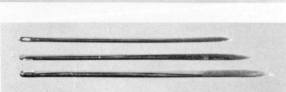

Fig. 26. Harness needles — used in hand sewing. Available in several sizes. Have egg eye and blunt point.

Fig. 27. Glover's needles — used in sewing lightweight leather. Available in several sizes. Have egg eye and three-square sharp point.

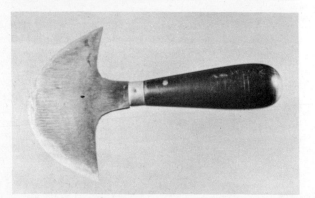

Fig. 28. Head knife — used for cutting heavy leather and for skiving.

Fig. 29. Swivel knife — used for cutting leather in carving.

Fig. 30. Saddle stamp — Used for decorating leather surfaces. See Fig. 145 and leathercraft catalogs for impressions of many other stamps.

Fig. 31. Striking stick — used for striking stamps. Varies in size and weight.

Fig. 32. Dividers — used to lay out circles and to space stitches and holes.

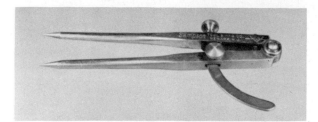

Fig. 33. Leather shears — used for cutting both light and heavy leather. A serrated blade prevents slipping of the leather.

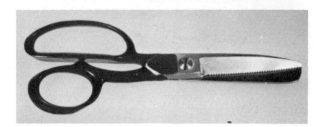

Fig. 34. Lacing pliers — used for pulling heavy lace and reaching ends of lace between layers when lacing is completed.

Fig. 35. Segma snap tool — used to set Segma snaps.

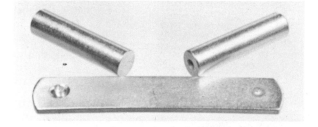

Fig. 36. Bissonnette edge tool — used to round off leather at edges. Sometimes called safety edger.

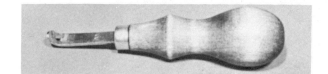

Fig. 37. Rampart gouger — used to cut grooves in heavy leather to aid in folding. Adjustable for depth of cut.

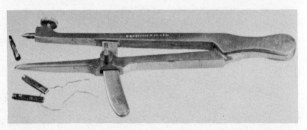

Fig. 38. Patent leather compasses — used for laying out and for cutting grooves for stitching. Has one point and three scratches.

Fig. 39. Lock stitch sewing awl — used to sew heavy leather with a lock stitch. Good for repair work.

Fig. 40. Oblong punch — used to punch holes for attaching buckles and bag straps. Available in several sizes.

Fig. 41. Skiving knife — used to skive leather.

Fig. 42. Skife — used to skive edges and to cut thin leather. Uses a Schick injector razor blade.

Fig. 43. English-point punch — used to cut a strap end to a point.

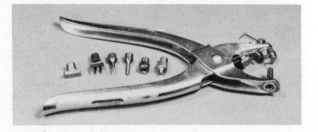

Fig. 44. Combination punch — a multipurpose tool with several attachments. Has a spacing gauge.

Craft leathers

A wide variety of leather is available for the craftsman. Craft leather comes in various weights and colors. The weight of leather is designated in ounces, with one-ounce leather being 1/64″ in thickness. Tooling and carving leather *must* be top grain, vegetable-tanned leather. See pages 137 to 139 for a brief description of "The Manufacture of Leather."

A brief description of craft leathers as to weights, uses, and sizes of the skins or sides follows. The illustrations show the grain of the various leathers in actual size.

Tooling and carving leathers

Fig. 45. Calf

Calf is an ideal tooling and carving leather for small projects. It comes in many colors as well as natural finish. The weight varies from 1½ to 3½ ounces. Skin size ranges from 9 to 16 square feet.

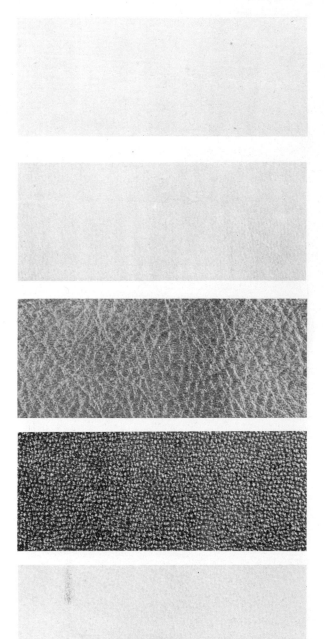

Fig. 46. Sheep

Sheep is an inexpensive leather which may be tooled. It is not so strong or durable as calf. Available in many colors, it generally comes in medium weight only. The size of skins varies from 7 to 12 square feet.

Fig. 47. Steerhide

Steerhide is a pebbly- or crinkly-grained pliable leather which tools very well. It may be used for all projects. It comes in natural or two-toned colors and varies in weight from 2½ to 5 ounces. The sides run from 20 to 28 square feet.

Fig. 48. Morocco goat

Morocco goat may be tooled. It is used for linings, billfolds, and book bindings. The weight is about 2½ ounces. The skins, varying in size up to 10 square feet, come in several colors.

Fig. 49. Pigskin

Pigskin may be tooled. It generally comes in natural color and is very tough and durable. The skins range from 9 to 16 square feet. The weight varies.

Fig. 50.   Cowhide

Carving cowhide or strap leather is ideal for both tooling and stamping. It may be used for all projects. It is natural in color and always has a smooth grain. The weight varies from 2½ to 10 ounces. The sides run up to 28 square feet.

Lining leathers

Fig. 51.   Chrome calf

Chrome calf cannot be tooled. Lightweight chrome calf makes an excellent smooth lining. It is available in several colors. The skins are from 7 to 12 square feet in size.

Fig. 52.   Skiver

Skiver is a very thin grain-split sheepskin. When used as a lining, it should be cemented solidly to the cover. It may be cemented to boxes for a covering. The skins are from 6 to 12 square feet, the color varying.

Fig. 53.   Suede

Suede is a type of finish. It is generally made on sheep in a wide range of colors. It is used for linings and garments. The skins average from 5 to 9 square feet.

Miscellaneous leathers

Fig. 54.   Alligator

Genuine alligator comes in several shades of mahogany and brown. It is used for billfolds and handbags. The skins vary in width from 6 to 14 inches. It is sold by the inch.

Fig. 55.   Lizard

Genuine lizard, available in several colors, is used for small projects. The skins are small, measuring from 8 to 11 inches in width.

Fig. 56. Ostrich

Genuine ostrich may be identified by the quill holes. The grain is often embossed upon cheaper leathers. The skins range in size up to 14 square feet.

Fig. 57. Alligator calf

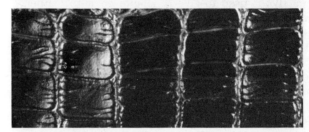

Alligator-grained calfskin may be used for most projects. A variety of colors is available. The skins may be as large as 14 square feet.

Fig. 58. Embossed cowhide

Embossed cowhide or steerhide is used for brief cases, notebooks, and other large projects. It is generally black or brown. The size of the sides ranges up to 28 square feet.

Fig. 59. Hair calf

Hair calf is calfskin with the hair still on it. The hair may be long or clipped. Unborn calf or slunk will have very short hair. It may be used for small projects and garments. The size of the skins is from 6 to 10 square feet.

Fig. 60. Lace

The commonly used widths of lace are ³⁄₃₂″ and ⅛″. Both goat and calf lace are available in several colors.

Dyes, finishes, and dressings

After the leathercraftsman has tooled, carved, or assembled his project, he should use one or more of the many leather finishes. Be careful—poor finishing may ruin what was up to that point a piece of good workmanship.

Two pieces of leather will not always receive a given dye uniformly because they differ in porosity and fiber structure. Tanning materials react differently to leather finishes. Different tanneries may use the same basic tanning processes, but they may use different chemical combinations to produce certain surface colors and finishes. All of this affects the final finish. Even parts of a single skin may react differently to various dyes.

Since there are so many variable factors, it is always necessary to test dyes or finishes on scrap leather. Be sure that the scrap leather used for testing is the same as the leather to be dyed. Follow the instruction in Operation 36, "How to Apply Finishes."

Dyes

A dye is used to give a definite color to leather, while a leather finish is applied over both natural and dyed areas to soften, protect, and condition the leather surface.

Oil and solvent dyes have been in general use for many years. The solvent dyes will penetrate more than oil dyes, but they give less gloss. Some dyes manufactured today have the desirable characteristics of both types of dyes.

Edge finishes

Several types of edge finishes may be used. Their purposes are to set and smooth the cut leather fibers and sometimes to color the leather.

Edges may be dyed to match or contrast with a surface color. A solvent edge dye will penetrate to a great depth and dry to a semi-gloss. Edge enamels have a resin base and may be thinned with water. They set the fibers in one application and dry to a high gloss. They do not penetrate so far as edge dyes. Waterproof edge enamels cannot be thinned with water. They are used on the edges of belts and watch straps to help prevent discoloration from perspiration.

Antique finishes

Antique finishes are used to beautify a carved design by bringing out a two-toned effect with high-lights and shadows. They are available in several colors but are not entirely waterproof and should be protected with a leather lacquer. Much experimenting should be done with this type of finish.

Protective finishes

After the project has been dyed, one of several finishes may be used to protect against perspiration, fingerprints, and dirt. Perhaps the best protective finish is a leather lacquer. It may be thinned with special lacquer thinner. One purpose of this finish is to preserve the color previously obtained when a dye was applied. Some leathers require a primer before lacquer is applied. This keeps the lacquer from flaking.

Resin finishes give a soft, satiny appearance to leather. They may be used as a primer on antique finishes before lacquer is applied. Wax finishes are often used to protect a dyed surface. They come in either liquid, stick, paste, or cake form. Liquid wax is used when a quick finish is needed. Stick wax of various blends may be almost pure carnauba wax which is applied by machine. Cake wax, which is usually pure beeswax, is applied to stitching thread.

Saddle soap is very good for cleaning leather which is not too dirty. It will soften the leather and restore natural oils. It may also be used as a base before dyes or lacquers are applied. Neatsfoot oil compound is used to soften and waterproof leather which will receive heavy and rough use. It will darken natural leather. Lexol is a liquid conditioner which restores the necessary oils to leather, thus preserving the fine appearance and extending the life of the leather article.

Tips on buying tools and supplies

Obtain one or more leathercraft catalogs before making tool and supply lists. Consult your classified telephone directory for leathercraft companies and check craft magazines for advertisements.

Tools

The suggested lists of tools on page 140 will aid you in determining the tools needed. If a tool is to be used often, it is economical to buy the best quality tool. As a general rule, good quality tools are the most economical for class use. It is never economical to buy a cheap revolving punch.

There are many kinds of needles which can be used in sewing leather. The common needle ("sharps" is the technical name) can be used to sew lightweight leather. Sharps vary in size from No. 1 to 12. They may be purchased at any notions counter. Glover's needles have a three-square sharp point. They vary in size from No. 000 to 7, with the larger number indicating the smaller needle. Harness needles have a blunt point. They, too, vary in size from No. 000 to 7. Most needles are bought by the package. Some packages contain an assortment of sizes.

When ordering tools, be sure to give the catalog number, the name of the tool, and its size if sizes are given. Some companies give a discount when tools are ordered in quantity.

Leather

The section on "The Manufacture of Leather" will explain how leather is split and how its thickness is measured. *All leather for tooling and carving must be top grain, vegetable-tanned leather.* Leathercraft supply companies will furnish this kind of leather.

A person starting in leathercraft may buy pre-cut projects. This is a saving if only a little work is to be done. For classwork it is better to buy whole skins or sides. A few companies will cut leather to the size of your project, but the cost is somewhat higher.

Supply companies differ in the way they sell leather. Some sell only whole skins, while others will sell half skins. See Fig. 61. Some companies will sell only full sides, while others may sell backs, bends, and shoulders. Leather which comes from the back of an animal has the best quality. Since it tools and carves well, it should be used for covers and parts which are to be tooled. The belly and leg sections are good leather also and should be used for gussets, pockets, and linings. See Fig. 62.

Various grades of leather are sold. Some companies sell only one grade, while others have two or three grades. The best grade is recommended for large projects. A lower grade may be used for small projects. There will be very little waste since the small patterns can be arranged on the leather so that the holes and other flaws can be cut out. An experienced leather worker knows that top grain leather will have some flaws or scratches on it. These marks are generally hidden after tooling or carving is completed. Do *not* insist upon a perfect piece of leather, for you can lay out the skin or side so that every inch of leather will be used for something.

Leather is sold by the square foot. In ordering leather, be sure to give the grade, kind, color, weight, and size of skin or side. Do *not* insist upon an exact number of feet in a skin or side, for the supply company may not have that exact size in stock. Quality is more important than an exact size. Check the company's current stock lists before ordering.

Other supplies

Order small amounts of leather finishes the first time. It may be that a particular finish does not meet your needs. After determining your needs, order in quantity lots.

All types of snaps, eyelets, dee rings, etc., are cheaper if ordered in quantity. Some companies

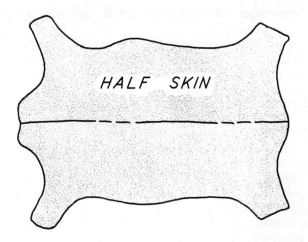

Fig. 61. A skin

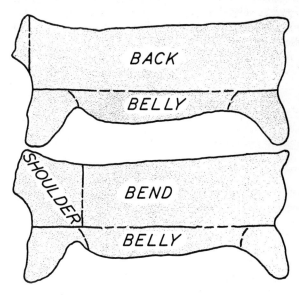

Fig. 62. Sides

give the sizes of snaps in lines, such as 10-line or 24-line. One line equals ¼₀″.

Obtain small amounts of heavy flax thread from a local shoe repairman. This thread may be six- or seven-cord. It may be waxed. A three- or four-cord thread is of medium weight. You may use No. 10 flax thread to make heavy thread for hand sewing. (See Operation 28.) Nylon thread is very strong. Sizes C and E are satisfactory for most machine or hand sewing. Heavy cotton thread is used on projects where strength is not important. Size C-30 is a lightweight thread; F-16 is heavy.

It is recommended that for beginners, either as individuals or as a class, only those supplies which will be used within a year be ordered. It is better to reorder than to have supplies on hand which will never be used.

Storage of leather and other craft supplies

The storage of leather and other supplies has always been a problem for both the individual craftsman and the instructor in a classroom. These few practical suggestions will help make more economical use of all leathercraft supplies.

Leather

Store leather in a clean, dry place. A warm, damp place may cause mildew to grow on the leather. Keep skins and sides flat on a large table if space permits, but very few craftsmen will have sufficient space to do this. If space for such storage is not available, roll the leather into a bundle with the grain side out. Then place the roll of leather on its side in a clean, dry place. Do *not* stand rolls of leather on end, for lightweight leathers will soon wrinkle where they rest on the floor. Roll lightweight leather around cardboard tubes to prevent the formation of wrinkles in it. Save all scrap pieces of leather, and use them for small projects. Many of them may be used for practice pieces for skiving, stamping, etc.

Other supplies

Never store dyes with leather. The dye bottles may be broken and the leather ruined. If dyes, finishes, and cement are bought in large quantities, pour some into small jars with good screw tops. Then use the small jars instead of opening up the large containers. This prevents evaporation and other waste. Label all jars.

Store all snap buttons, eyelets, and rivets in small glass bottles or jars. (See Fig. 78.) In this way, a quick and easy selection of a small article may be made. Label each container. Use surplus supplies to replenish the small bottles whenever it is necessary.

FUNDAMENTAL

OPERATIONS

The "How-to-Do" section
of this book is well illustrated.
Always read the entire operation
and study the illustrations
before working. Then carefully follow
the step-by-step procedure
in doing the work.

Operation 1   How to design a project

Designing is a subject in itself and should be taught as such. In the designing of a project, the size, shape, material, and method of decoration should all be considered. Space does not permit us to consider the primary principles of design.

In this book are many projects which have been designed for you. They have actually been made by following the step-by-step procedures. *All allowances have been made in the layout drawings.*

If you are a beginner in leathercraft, it is recommended that you select a small project from this book for your first attempt to work with leather. After you become familiar with leather and the tools used to work it, you may want to design a project for yourself. You will derive much pride and satisfaction from developing an original design. The following practical suggestions will help you to develop your own leather articles and decorative designs.

Procedure for the project

1. Study leather articles illustrated in catalogs, magazines, and newspapers or those displayed in stores.

2. Lay out on heavy paper each part of the project. Use crosshatched paper as an aid in laying out a curved or irregular line. Such paper is also helpful in decreasing or increasing the size of a project or a design.

3. To get an accurate project pattern, make all necessary allowances. See Fig. 63. Add the thickness of the leather to the length of each piece for each

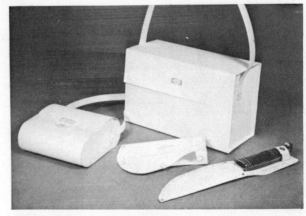

Fig. 64. Paper models of projects

Fig. 65. Determining the size of an ax sheath

bend, A. Add the thickness of the part where the leather overlaps, B. Add twice the thickness of the leather for folds where they are made, C.

4. In sewing or lacing gussets to a cover, add the thickness of the leather to the width of each piece as shown at D, Fig. 63. On heavy leather, add ¼″ to each piece if it is to be sewed as shown at E, Fig. 63.

5. Add all allowances to the paper pattern. Then construct the project from the paper pattern. Make the folds in the paper where the folds will come in the leather. Fasten the corners or gussets with cellophane tape, paper clips, or by sewing.

6. Mark the locations for fasteners, sewing, and lacing.

7. Make all necessary changes on the paper model as to size and shape. Since this may be the cutting pattern later on, it must be accurate. See Fig. 64.

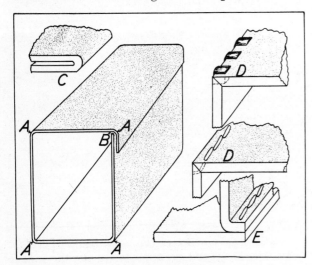

Fig. 63. Determining allowances in a pattern

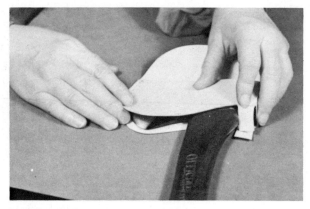

Fig. 66. Checking the size of a pattern

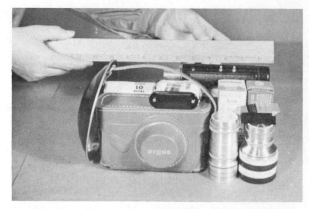

Fig. 67. Determining the size of a gadget bag

Ax sheath

8. Determine the size of an ax sheath or gun holster by laying the ax or gun upon heavy paper and tracing around it with a pencil. Be sure to make allowance for the thickness of the article and for sewing or lacing. See Fig. 65.

9. Cut out the pattern. Fold it around the article to check that it is the correct size. See Fig. 66.

10. You may design patterns without gussets for many different objects in this way.

Gadget bag

11. Determine the size of a gadget bag by assembling all articles which you will carry in it. You may need to rearrange these articles several times to determine the best size and shape. See Fig. 67.

12. Construct the bag from heavy paper. If they are desired, attach pockets for film, lenses, light meter, etc., to the inside with cement or cellophane tape.

13. Locate the positions for the handles, lock, or strap.

Field glasses case

14. In designing a pattern for a case for something like field glasses, place heavy paper around the object as shown in Fig. 68. Make the cover approximately ¼″ wider than the object to allow for the gussets or end pieces.

15. Decide upon the type of fastener for the flap, either a strap or a case lock. Determine how the carrying strap will be attached to the case. Locate the positions of these parts on the pattern.

Procedure for the decorative design

16. If the project is to be tooled or carved, check the pattern to see how much space will admit decoration. You must make allowances for the lacing on the edges, for folds, and for fasteners.

17. The design should be as simple as possible for a beginner. More difficult problems may be undertaken as you gain skill and experience. In outline

Fig. 68. Determining case size for field glasses

Fig. 69. Copying a design

tooling, the design should consist mainly of straight lines.

18. Select a design which will fill the area you wish to decorate. Choose one from the back of this book or from one of the many books of designs. The design should be appropriate for the kind of tooling, carving, or decorating to be done.

19. Place a piece of tracing paper, which is a transparent paper, (*not* carbon) over the design selected. Copy the design. Be sure to use a soft pencil.

Fig. 70.   Shading to aid in transferring a design

Fig. 71.   Pattern with a design

Copying designs in this way will not destroy the paper in the book. See Fig. 69.

20. Shade the under side of the copied design with a soft pencil. See Fig. 70. The shaded side will aid in transferring the design from the tracing paper to the paper pattern of your project.

The design may be traced directly upon the leather from the tracing paper. If this is done, do *not* shade the under side of the tracing paper. *Never* use carbon paper around leather.

21. Check the design to see that it is correct in every detail. In outline tooling, you will need only an outline. In flat modeling and carving, shade the background of the design. See Fig. 71. In embossing, highlight that portion of the design which is to be embossed.

22. Learn to develop your own decorative designs by studying the many designs which are available. Use tracing paper. Adapt parts of several designs to a given area. Reverse the design, and you will develop many new combinations. Use compasses to develop flowers for carving. Designs for carving should have very little background.

Operation 2   How to make templates

Templates are patterns used to lay out work, to aid in cutting stock, or to check the accuracy of work. They prevent waste of material and increase accuracy in getting out stock.

Procedure for temporary templates

1. You may use the paper patterns made in Operation 1 for temporary templates.

2. Make a more durable template by laying out the pattern on heavy cardboard or cementing the pattern to cardboard. Check the layout for correct size and shape.

3. Cut out the template, using tin snips or heavy scissors. Label the template.

4. Fasten ¾″ cellophane tape to the edges of cardboard templates to make smoother edges and prevent wear on the cardboard. Place the tape upon the edge of the cardboard as shown in Fig. 72. Smooth down the tape along both sides of the edge. See the insert in Fig. 72.

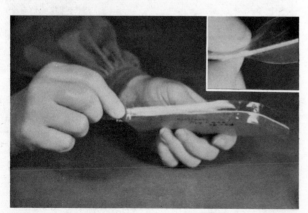

Fig. 72.   Taping the edge of a cardboard template

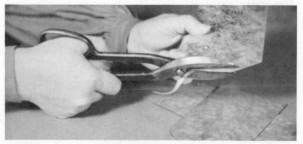

Fig. 73.   Cutting a template with tin snips

Procedure for permanent templates

5. Lay out the pattern on 28-gauge galvanized iron with a scratch awl. Check the layout for correct size and shape. Permanent templates should be made whenever a project is to be made several times.

6. Cut out the template, using tin snips as shown in Fig. 73.

7. File all edges to remove burrs. Use steel wool to smooth the edges so that the metal will not scratch the leather.

8. Label the templates, using paint or India ink. See Fig. 74.

Fig. 74. Templates

Operation 3 How to lay out

Read page 19 for information on the various qualities of leather to be found in a single skin.

Procedure

1. Move the templates, both temporary and permanent, around in order to utilize the skin to the best advantage. See Fig. 75. Remember that the back of the skin is the best quality. Use it for covers or parts that will be tooled. Use the legs and belly sections for gussets, pockets, and linings.

2. Keep one edge of the skin or side straight in order to cut long pieces for gussets. Use a long straightedge such as a yardstick to lay out this straight edge.

3. If a square is used, see that its edges are smooth so that it will not scratch the leather. Use an awl to mark the leather where it is to be cut. See Fig. 76. Mark the leather *only* where it is to be cut.

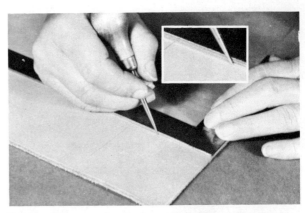

Fig. 76. Using an awl and square to lay out

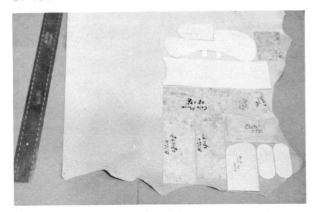

Fig. 75. Templates arranged on a skin

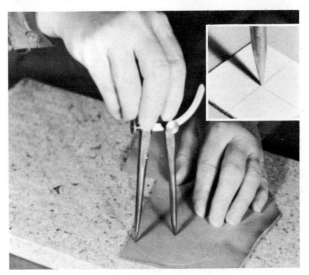

Fig. 77. Using dividers to lay out a circle

4. You may use a pencil to lay out dimensions on natural leather.

5. Use compasses or dividers to lay out circles. See Fig. 77.

6. Place a small piece of cardboard at the center of a circle to protect the leather from the point of the compasses or dividers. See the insert in Fig. 77.

7. Use an awl to trace around paper and metal templates.

Operation 4   How to store, sharpen, and condition tools

A good craftsman will have a good place to store his tools. This will prevent damage to the tools not in use and help to keep them in first-class condition. The most important thing in cutting leather is to have a sharp knife. A dull knife causes ninety per cent of a beginner's trouble in working with leather.

Procedure for storage

1. Make racks to hold all tools in wall cabinets or individual tool kits. The storage place should be compact. See Figs. 78 and 79. Fig. 79 shows the author's tool kit which contains a complete assortment of tools.

2. Place sharp tools so that their edges will not be damaged and no person will be injured.

3. Make small kits from lightweight leather or flannel for stamping tools. See Fig. 80.

Procedure for sharpening

4. As a rule, you do not need to grind the cutting edges of knives. Sharpen them by whetting them on a clean oilstone. Use a coarse stone first, then a finer one. Apply a small amount of oil to the stone.

5. Hold the blade of a skiving knife against the stone at the angle at which the blade is ground. See Fig. 81. Apply pressure when the direction of the stroke is toward the cutting edge. Whet both sides of the blade. Clean the stone with a cloth.

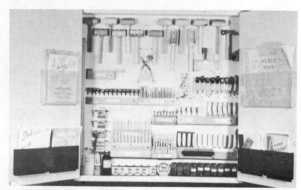

Fig. 78.   Tool cabinet for a class

Fig. 79.   Individual tool box

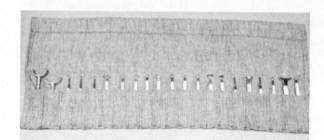

Fig. 80.   Stamping tool kit

Fig. 81.   Whetting a skiving knife

6. Starting at one point of the blade, whet the head knife, using a circular motion. See Fig. 82. Turn the handle slightly as you sharpen the blade around to the other point. Sharpen both sides of the blade.

7. Whet the swivel knife on both sides in a back-and-forth motion. See Fig. 83. Be sure to hold the knife at the angle the blade is ground. Keep the blade at this angle. Refrain from rocking it.

8. Since the blade of the swivel knife must be sharp, smooth, and polished, whet it next on a piece of crocus cloth. Place the crocus cloth upon a flat surface. See Fig. 84.

9. Strop the swivel knife on a rouge board. Make a rouge board by gluing a 1½″ x 9″ piece of 6- to 8-oz. strap leather, grain side up, to ¼″ plywood. Rub jeweler's rouge into the leather. Use the grain side of a piece of strap leather if a rouge board is not available. Pull the blade across the leather in one direction only. See Fig. 85. Lift the blade between strokes so that you will not cut the leather strop. Be sure to wipe the rouge off the knife before you cut leather with it.

10. Strop the edges of all knives if a keener edge is desired. Remember to pull the blade across the leather, lifting it between strokes so that you will not cut the strop.

11. Sharpen a thonging chisel by whetting it on an oilstone. Hold it at the angle at which the prongs are ground. See Fig. 86.

12. Sharpen an awl by pulling it along the surface of an oilstone at the angle at which it is ground. Revolve the awl between the fingers as you pull it over the oilstone. See Fig. 87.

Fig. 84. Whetting a swivel knife on crocus cloth

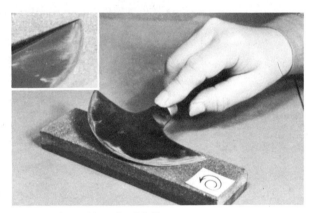

Fig. 82. Sharpening a head knife

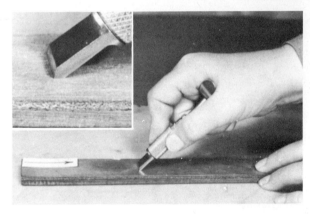

Fig. 85. Stropping a swivel knife on a rouge board

Fig. 83. Whetting a swivel knife

Fig. 86. Whetting a thonging chisel

13. Sharpen a drive punch by holding it almost parallel with the oilstone. See Fig. 88. Rotate the drive punch as you pull it across the stone, thus whetting the cutting edge.

14. Sharpen the tubes of a revolving punch by using a medium abrasive cloth. Place the punch in a vise. Pull the abrasive cloth back and forth as you move it around a tube. See Fig. 89.

15. Sharpen a common edger on a piece of fine emery cloth. Wrap the emery cloth around a dowel

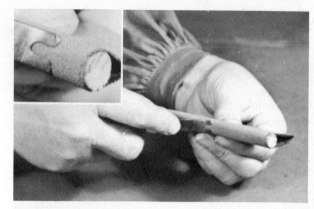

Fig. 90.   Sharpening an edger

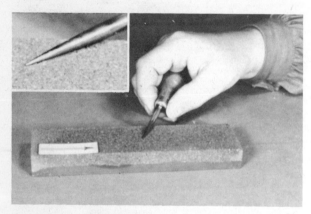

Fig. 87.   Sharpening an awl

Fig. 91.   Polishing the end of a modeler

Fig. 88.   Whetting a drive punch

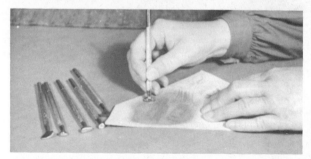

Fig. 92.   Conditioning the end of a stamp

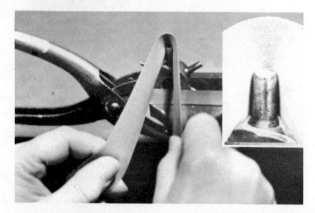

Fig. 89   Sharpening a tube of a revolving punch

Fig. 93.   Sawing end of rawhide mallet

Fig. 94.   Mallets, before and after reconditioning

Fig. 95.   Filing the anvil of a revolving punch

rod or any other rounded object which fits the curvature of the edger. Move the edger back and forth over the emery cloth, thus whetting it. See Fig. 90. Be sure to hold the edger against the emery cloth at the angle at which it was ground.

Procedure for conditioning

16. Use crocus cloth to polish the ends of modelers if they become nicked or scratched. See Fig. 91.

17. New saddle stamps may have particles of the plating embedded in the design part of the stamp. Place the stamp upon a piece of practically dry strap leather. Strike it with a mallet, using medium force. This should remove the particles of plating from the stamp.

18. Both smooth and lined stamps may be reconditioned by rubbing them over a piece of leather which has had jeweler's rouge applied to the surface. See Fig. 92. Remove all rouge from the stamps before using them.

19. Rawhide mallets which have been badly worn through long use may be reconditioned. Place the mallet in a vise as shown in Fig. 93. Cut off a thin slice with a backsaw, thus squaring up the face of the mallet. Sand the surface after the end has been cut off. Fig. 94 shows two mallet heads, one before and one after reconditioning.

20. If the anvil of a revolving punch has become rough, file it down smooth with a mill file. See Fig. 95. The insert in Fig. 95 shows two punch anvils, one having been reconditioned, the other not.

Operation 5   How to cut leather

The first requirement for cutting leather is a sharp knife. Sharpen the knife as given in Operation 4. A good cutting board is also essential. Soft pine makes an excellent cutting board since the grain will not deflect the knife as the leather is cut. Be sure to check all templates and layouts for accuracy before the leather is cut.

Procedure

1. Cut along the edge of a square with a bevel point knife. Hold the knife at about a 45 degree angle to the leather. Hold the square firmly so that it will not slip. See Fig. 96.

2. Cut around a template with a knife. Use enough pressure to cut through the leather on the first stroke. Do *not* cut past a corner as shown in Fig. 97. Stop the blade about 1/16″ from the corner.

Reverse the direction of the blade by placing it directly at the corner and completing the cut as

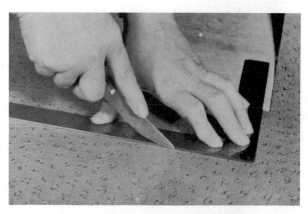

Fig. 96.   Using a square and knife to cut leather

shown in Fig. 98. This method eliminates waste of leather.

3. Cut heavy leather with a head knife. To cut small pieces, extend the leather over the edge of a table. Hold the knife as shown in Fig. 99. Push it along the pattern line.

4. To cut large pieces of heavy leather, raise from the table only that part of the leather which is to be cut. Use the knife as shown in Fig. 100. You may also use the knife as shown in Fig. 101.

5. Use leather shears to cut both light and heavy leather. Their serrated blade prevents slipping of the leather. They are especially good for cutting along curved and irregular lines. See Fig. 102.

6. Cut long straps of leather with the draw gauge. Before it is used, cut one edge of a hide straight

Fig. 97.   Do not cut past the corner of a template

Fig. 100.   Cutting large pieces with a head knife

Fig. 98.   Correct way to complete a corner cut

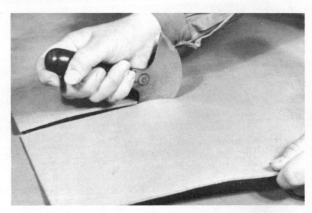

Fig. 101.   Alternate way to hold head knife

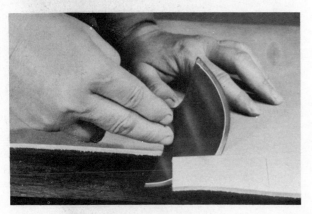

Fig. 99.   Cutting small pieces with a head knife

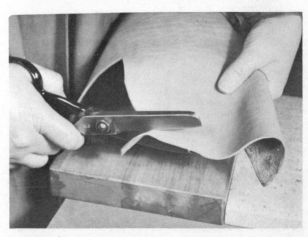

Fig. 102.   Using leather shears

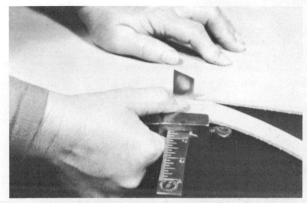

Fig. 103. Cutting a strap with a draw gauge

Fig. 104. Cutting leather with a paper cutter

by using a skiving or head knife. Set the draw gauge for the width desired. Hold the draw gauge as shown in Fig. 103. Pull it toward you, thus

cutting the strap. Hold the ends of small pieces of leather in a vise, or clamp or nail them to a table top.

7. Use a paper cutter to cut lightweight leather along straight lines. See Fig. 104.

Operation 6 — How to moisten leather for tooling and carving

Tooling and carving leather *must* be top grain, vegetable-tanned leather. It will not hold a good impression unless it is made pliable by moisture. All leathers differ as to the amount of water and time necessary to prepare them for tooling.

Procedure for lightweight leather

1. Cut out the pieces of the project. Operations 3 and 5.

2. Remove any dust from the grain side with a damp cloth.

3. Moisten lightweight leather on the flesh side with a clean sponge and cold water. See Fig. 105. When the finished side darkens, the proper moisture content has been reached. Moisten the entire piece of leather so that any shrinkage or color change will be uniform.

4. Place the leather upon a flat surface, grain side up. Let it dry until the surface begins to resume its original color. It is then ready to have the design traced on it.

Fig. 105. Moistening leather with a sponge

Procedure for heavy leather

5. Scrub heavy strap leather with a soft bristle brush and mild soap. See Fig. 106. This will remove any dirt or sand which may be in the pores of the hide.

6. Rinse all traces of soap from the leather.

7. Soak the leather in water for a few minutes. Then cover it or wrap it in a towel for several

Fig. 106. Scrubbing strap leather

Fig. 107. Leather stored in plastic bags

hours or even overnight. This causes the fiber bundles to swell and makes the leather very soft and pliable. This preparation is called *casing* the leather. It is a very important step in properly preparing leather for carving.

8. Place the leather upon a flat surface grain side up. Let it dry until the surface shows traces of its original color. It is then ready to have the design transferred to it.

9. It may not be necessary to case some strap leathers as given in step 7. Moisten them on both the grain and flesh sides. If they do not cut easily, proceed as in step 7.

10. You must be very careful in handling leather once it has been moistened, for it will take any impression imposed upon it. Even fingernails may leave marks.

11. If work cannot be completed in one day, place the leather in a plastic bag or wrap it in waxed paper to retain the correct moisture content. See Fig. 107.

12. If work must be held over for several days in warm weather, wrap the leather in waxed paper or a plastic bag and refrigerate it. This will prevent mildew.

Operation 7   How to make design templates

Design templates speed up the transferring of decorative designs to leather. They are used for production work and for repeated designs such as in belts.

Fig. 108. Drying a template

Fig. 109. Design templates

Procedure

1. Prepare a piece of 8- to 10-oz. strap leather for carving. (Operation 6.)

2. Transfer the design to the leather. (Operation 8.) The design on the template will be imposed upon the leather in reverse. You must consider this in developing designs for templates if the reversal of the design will be noticeable.

3. Cut the design with a swivel knife. (Operation 15.)

4. Dry the leather in an oven at 150 degrees. The heat will tend to harden the leather and open up the cuts. If the template is to be used only a few times, this step is not necessary.

5. If an oven is not available, you may use a 100-watt bulb and a reflector to dry the leather. See Fig. 108. For a temperature of about 140 degrees, place the reflector about five inches away from the template.

6. Waterproof the template with a leather finisher or a coat of shellac. Fig. 109 shows completed belt templates.

Operation **8**   How to transfer designs to leather

Check the design to see that it is complete and correct in every detail. After a design has been transferred to the leather, it is almost impossible to remove any lines. *Never* use carbon paper to transfer a design to leather.

Procedure for tracing patterns

1. Prepare the leather for tooling or carving. (Operation 6.)

2. Place the tracing pattern upon the grain side of the leather. Fasten it to the leather with cellophane or masking tape. Place the tape along the edge of the pattern. Bring the tape down over the leather, fastening it to the flesh side. See the center design in Fig. 110.

3. Alternate ways to hold a design pattern to leather are: paper clips spread apart somewhat so that they will not mark the leather; thumb tacks or push pins pushed down through the design pattern and waste portion of the leather; or, on large projects, weights placed upon the design pattern and leather to keep them from moving.

4. Place the leather and design pattern upon a smooth, firm surface such as a piece of marble, plate glass, or hard wood. You should never use plate glass when you are stamping leather, but it does make a good surface for tracing or tooling. Use a tracing tool, pencil, the small end of a modeler, or a stylus to trace the design. See Fig. 111. If you use a pencil, be careful that it does not go through the paper and mark the leather. Use a firm, even pressure as you trace the design.

5. Always use a straightedge to aid in tracing straight lines. See Fig. 112.

6. Raise one end of the design occasionally to see that the leather is taking a clear impression of the design and that you have not missed any lines. See Fig. 113.

Procedure for design templates

7. Place the design template upon the properly prepared leather with the design side against the grain side of the leather. Pound the back of the template with a smooth-faced mallet. See Fig. 114.

The outline of the design will be slightly raised

Fig. 111.   Tracing a design

Fig. 112.   Using a straightedge for straight lines

Fig. 113.   Checking a design tracing

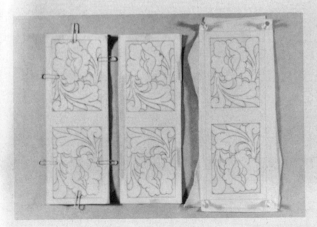

Fig. 110.   Design patterns fastened to leather

above the surface of the moist leather and will be reversed from that on the template.

8. As an alternate way to transfer a design with a template, place the leather and template between two boards. Apply pressure with a bookpress or vise. See Fig. 115.

Fig. 114. Using a design template

9. In using a design template for a repeated design, be sure that the template is placed upon the leather to match the design already transferred. In some patterns the design may be continuous, but in others you may have to turn the template end-for-end to make the design continuous.

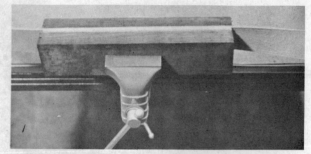

Fig. 115. Using a vise to transfer a belt design

Operation 9 How to do outline tooling

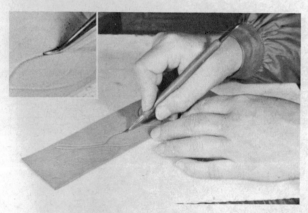

Fig. 116. Correct way to hold a modeler

In outline tooling only the outline of the design is pressed down. This is one of the simplest ways to decorate leather. The bookmark at the top in Fig. 296 shows outline tooling.

Procedure

1. Transfer the design. (Operation 8.)
2. Place the leather upon a marble slab. Go over the outline of the design several times with the small end of a modeler until the lines are depressed to the desired depth. Hold the modeler as you would a pencil. See Fig. 116. Increase the pressure as you go over the design. Be sure that you keep the depth of the depressed lines uniform.

Fig. 117. Tooling a straight line

Fig. 118. Using the Vibro-Tool for outline tooling

3. If water oozes up back of the modeler, let the leather dry a little. Leather which is too damp will not hold an impression. If the modeler tends to scratch or break through the surface of the leather, dampen the leather a little on the grain side with a sponge. Dry leather will not take a good impression.

4. Use a straightedge to aid in tooling all straight lines. See Fig. 117. Do *not* try to tool straight lines freehand. To prevent stretching lightweight leather, tool straight lines from the outer edges toward the center of the piece of leather.

5. You may use a Vibro-Tool for outline tooling. Fit the tool with a 1/16" round-nosed hammer. Use a small needle with a rounded point for fine work. Hold the tool as shown in Fig. 118. The insert in Fig. 118 shows an initialed bag plate made with the Vibro-Tool.

Operation 10 — How to do flat modeling

In flat modeling the background is depressed or beveled down away from the design, thus making the design stand out in bold relief. See Fig. 119.

Procedure

1. Transfer the design. (Operation 8.)

2. Go over the design as in outline tooling. (Operation 9.)

3. Depress or bevel the background around the design by using the broad end of the modeler as shown in Fig. 120.

4. The deerfoot modeler may be used for putting down background. See Fig. 121. Use a firm, even pressure.

5. The Vibro-Tool may be fitted with a flat-nosed hammer and used to put down the background. Hold the tool in a vertical position. See Fig. 122. Move it slowly back and forth over the leather.

6. Soften the edges of the design by using the broad end of the modeler to smooth them off.

7. If the leather becomes too dry, use a sponge to moisten it slightly on the grain side.

8. Read Operation 12 for information on background enrichment.

Fig. 119. Billfold

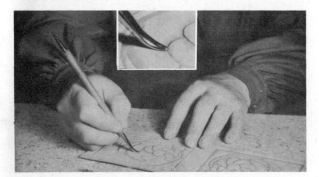

Fig. 120. Beveling background with a modeler

Fig. 121. Using the deerfoot modeler

Fig. 122. Putting down background with the Vibro-Tool

Operation 11   How to do embossing

Embossing is raising the design, or a part of it, above the surface of the leather by working from the flesh side. See Fig. 123.

Procedure

1. Transfer the design. (Operation 8.)

2. Go over the design as in outline tooling. This will give a clear outline of the design on the flesh side. (Operation 9.)

3. Hold the work in one hand with the flesh side up. Using the ball-end modeler, raise the design by rubbing the tool over the flesh side of the leather and forcing it down between the two fingers which hold that portion of the leather which is to be embossed. See Fig. 124.

4 Place the flesh side of the leather upon a piece of marble. Smooth down the background around the embossed part of the design. See Fig. 125. Repeat steps 3 and 4 until the design is raised to the desired height.

5. As an alternate way to work the leather in embossing, place it grain side down upon a piece of sponge rubber. Emboss the design by forcing the leather down into the rubber, using modelers.

6. Study Operation 12 for background enrichment.

7. After the leather has dried, back the embossed parts with either kapok or bits of newspapers. See Fig. 126. Mix the kapok with flour and water. Then place it into the back of the design, filling in level with the background. As an alternate method, use small bits of newspaper and rubber cement to fill in the back of the embossed areas.

8. Cement a lining to the flesh side of the leather after the backing is thoroughly dry.

Fig. 123.   Embossed book end

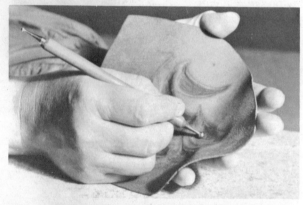

Fig. 124.   Embossing with the ball-end modeler

Fig. 125.   Putting down background in embossing

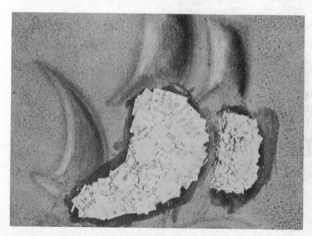

Fig. 126.   Backing embossed areas

Operation 12   How to stipple backgrounds

Stippling is decorating with small dot-like impressions. Stippling backgrounds accentuates the design. Many tools may be used for stippling.

Procedure

1. Have the leather in the same condition as for tooling.

2. Use a tracer, stylus, or the small end of a modeler for fine stippling. See Fig. 127. Be careful not to break through the outer surface of the leather.

3. Hold the ball-end modeler in a vertical position. See Fig. 128. Turn it as you apply pressure.

4. The stippler shown in Fig. 18 is faster to use since it covers a greater area. Hold it vertically. See Fig. 129. Be sure to apply uniform pressure.

5. Fit the Vibro-Tool with a round-nosed hammer. Hold it vertically, lifting the tool just enough to clear the leather after each impression. See Fig. 130. Practice on scrap leather.

Fig. 127.   Stippling with a modeler

Fig. 129.   Using a stippler

Fig. 128.   Stippling with a ball-end modeler

Fig. 130.   Stippling with a Vibro-Tool

Operation 13   How to use the embossing wheel and carriage

The embossing wheel and carriage is used to decorate borders. Its use may be incorporated into the design itself. The carriage has interchangeable embossing wheels. See Fig. 131.

Procedure

1. Have the leather in the same condition as for tooling.

2. Lay out the lines to be embossed.

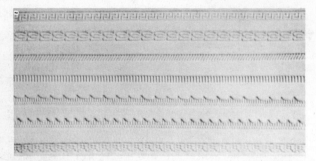

Fig. 131. Embossed lines

3. Hold the carriage as shown in Fig. 132. Push it along a straightedge. Be sure to apply enough pressure to leave a clear impression the first time over the leather since it is impossible to go over the line a second time.

4. Emboss curved lines by using a cardboard template or by doing them freehand. See Fig. 133.

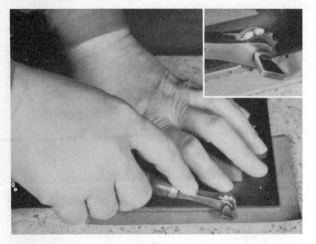

Fig. 132. Embossing a straight line

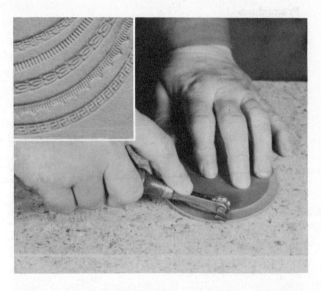

Fig. 133. Embossing a curved line

Operation 14   How to do set stamping

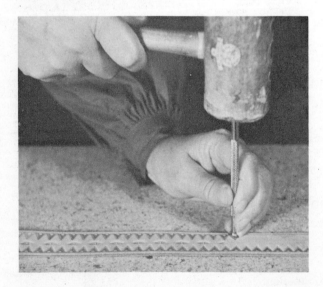

Fig. 134. Correct way to hold a stamp

Set stamping is using stamping tools without first cutting the leather with a swivel knife. It is one of the simplest ways to decorate leather. Children in the lower grades can use this method. Simple or very complicated designs may be developed. Craft catalogs list many stamps suitable for this type of decoration.

Procedure

1. Prepare the project leather and also some scrap leather as for tooling. (Operation 6.)

2. When the grain side of the leather has returned to its natural color, stamp the design first upon some scrap leather. Place the leather upon a piece of marble.

3. Hold the stamp vertically between the thumb and first and second fingers with the other fingers resting on the leather as shown in Fig. 134.

4. Strike the stamp sharply with a mallet. Do not cut through the leather with the stamping tool.

5. Use the edge creaser on belts before stamping is done. (Operation 17.) Fig. 135 shows a few belts decorated with set stamping.

6. Fill in or decorate large areas with set stamping. See Fig. 136. The basket stamp is very good for this sort of decoration.

7. Use geometric, border, and many other stamps for border decoration. Various designs may be developed. See Fig. 137.

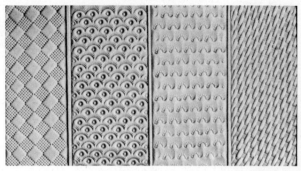

Fig. 136. Set stamping for large areas

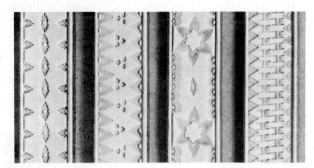

Fig. 135. Stamped belts

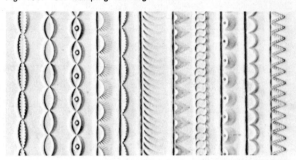

Fig. 137. Border stamping

Operation 15   How to do carving

Leather carving is the process of cutting a design into leather. No leather is actually cut away or removed. Saddle stamps are used to put down the background and to decorate the design. This method of decorating leather is sometimes called incising, stamping, or tooling.

In carving there is no definite set procedure which must be followed. However, the leather must always be in the best possible condition for carving. Every leather carver has his own method and style of carving, but the fundamental principles remain the same. To become proficient at carving requires much practice.

Read and follow all directions carefully.

General instructions

1. You may carve unglazed cowhide, tooling calf, goat, or sheep.

2. Use *only* top grain, vegetable-tanned leather.

3. If you are a beginner, you should not use leather lighter than four ounce.

All panels for the progressive steps in this operation and for the carved projects in this book were hand-carved by Ken Griffin. He is a nationally known leather carver who has written several publications on carving. See the Reference List on page 142.

4. Cowhide is firmer and tougher than other carving leathers; therefore, you can strike the stamps harder.

5. Practice on scrap pieces of various weights and kinds of leather. Vary the moisture content of the leather.

6. The swivel knife may be adjustable or nonadjustable. (See Fig. 29 in the section on "Tools and Supplies.") The adjustable knife enables the craftsman to adjust its length to the size of his hand. Use a ⅜" or ½" blade.

7. The angle of the cutting edge may vary from 50 to 80 degrees. Use the large-angle blade on lightweight leather and the narrow one on heavy leather and for making fine dress cuts. Since you cut to one-half the thickness of the leather, the widths of the cuts made by the two blades will be about the same. See Fig. 138. Most blades are about 70 degrees. The beginner needs only this blade.

Procedure in cutting the design

8. Prepare the leather for carving. (Operation 6.)

9. When the surface of the leather resumes its original color, transfer the design to the leather. (Operation 8.)

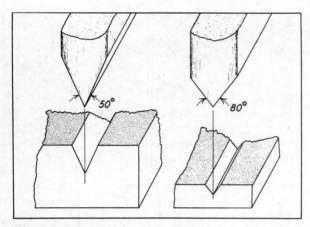

Fig. 138. Angles of swivel knife blades

10. After the design has been transferred, use a sponge to moisten the grain surface of the leather. It must be almost wet for cutting the design.

11. Be sure the swivel knife is sharp. (Read steps 7, 8, and 9 in Operation 4.) A dull knife tends to drag as you cut the leather. Strop the blade frequently on a rouge board.

12. Hold the knife with the first finger over the yoke and the knurled barrel between the thumb, second, and third fingers with the little finger along the side of the blade as shown in Fig. 139. An alternate way to hold the knife is to have the knurled barrel between the thumb and second finger as shown in Fig. 140. Relax! Use the method which is natural for you.

13. Practice making cuts on prepared scrap leather, holding the knife by either method. Pull the knife toward you along the traced design outline. Change the direction of the blade by rotating the

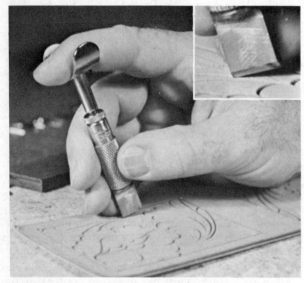

Fig. 139. A good way to hold the swivel knife

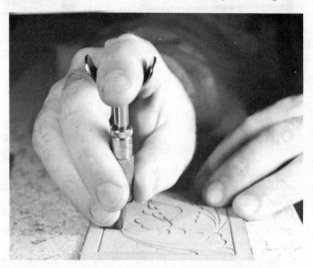

Fig. 141. Holding the swivel knife at a right angle

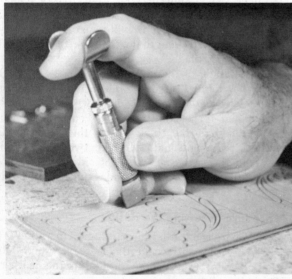

Fig. 140. An alternate way to hold the knife

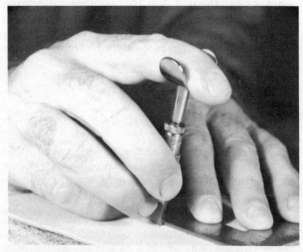

Fig. 142. Cutting a straight line with a swivel knife

knurled barrel between the thumb and second and even the third finger. Let the little finger glide over the leather. Make all cuts at right angles to the surface of the leather. Fig. 141 shows the knife held at a right angle to the leather.

14. Finish each cut by gradually lifting the knife, producing a cut which is shallow at the end. The insert in Fig. 139 shows the completion of a cut.

15. Use a straightedge as an aid in cutting straight lines. Pull the knife along the straightedge as shown in Fig. 142.

16. You may use the pro-gauge to aid in cutting

irregular border lines if the leather is cut to the correct size. See Fig. 143.

17. Cut the design in the following order: border lines, flowers, stems, and leaves. Make the cuts about one-half the thickness of the leather.

18. You should *never* do the following things: go over a cut a second time; cut across another cut; undercut; cut deeper than one-half the thickness of the leather; use a dull knife; or cut dry leather.

19. If you have not made smooth, even cuts, the knife may be dull or the leather not properly conditioned. If the blade tends to pull as you cut, strop the blade. Fig. 144 shows a billfold design completely cut.

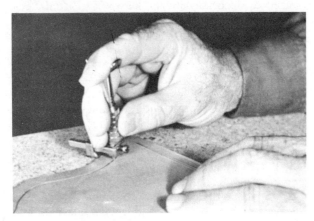

Fig. 143. Using the pro-gauge

Fig. 144. A design completely cut

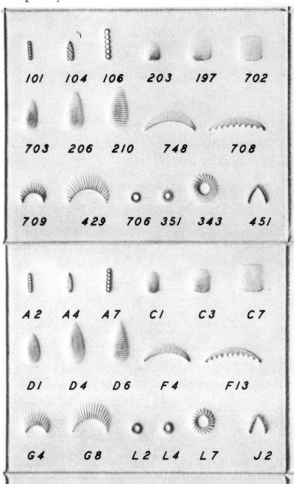

Fig. 145. Impressions of Craftool and Osborne stamps

No. 101 or A2 — background tool
No. 104 or A4 — background tool
No. 106 or A7 — background tool
No. 203 or C1 — smooth small beveler
No. 197 or C3 — smooth beveler
No. 702 or C7 — fine checked beveler

No. 703 or D1 — smooth shader
No. 206 or D4 — smooth shader
No. 210 or D6 — ribbed horizontal shader
No. 748 or F4 — shell
No. 708 or F13 — veiner
No. 709 or G4 — camouflage
No. 429 or G8 — camouflage
No. 706 or L2 — seeder
No. 351 or L4 — seeder
No. 343 or L7 — seeder
No. 451 or J2 — mule foot

Procedure in stamping the design

20. Study the impressions of the various stamps shown in Fig. 145. The stamps with only a number are Craftool Company's stamps. Those with both a letter and a number are the C. S. Osborne Company's stamps.

21. A minimum list of tools needed for carving by an individual as well as a recommended list for a class will be found on page 140. Check a catalog for a complete list of stamps. Only the more important stamps will be used in the progressive stamping which follows.

22. For stamping, the grain side of the leather must be almost dry. If the surface is dry and the leather moist under the surface, the tool impressions will be dark, which is what you want. Wet leather will not hold an impression of a tool, while dry leather will not even take an impression. Moisten the leather slightly on the grain side if it is necessary.

Camouflage

This stamp comes in several sizes and shapes. It is used to decorate flowers, leaves, and stems. See impressions numbered 709, 429, G4, and G8 in Fig. 145.

23. Hold the camouflage tool with the thumb, first, and second fingers. Let the third and little fingers rest on the leather. The stamp should not quite touch the leather. See Fig. 146.

24. Strike the stamp with a mallet or striking stick, holding as shown in Fig. 146. Use a wrist motion for the average stamping with the elbow resting on the table. After you strike the stamp, it will spring back to the holding position given in step 23. Your fingers act as springs.

25. Space the impressions uniformly, beginning the base of leaves, stems, and petals. See Fig. 147. Use less striking force as you progress toward the tips.

Pear shader

This tool also comes in several sizes. It may be smooth, checked, or ribbed. Use it to produce a shaded effect on leaves and flower petals. See impressions 703, D4, and D6 in Fig. 145.

26. Hold the shader as instructed in step 23 except that this tool may sometimes be tilted slightly in order to produce tapering depressions. See Fig. 148. Depress the leather uniformly away from the swivel knife cuts. See Fig. 149.

27. Move or push a smooth shader along as you strike it, producing a smooth, tapered depression.

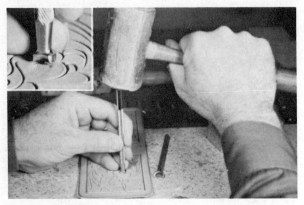

Fig. 146. Holding a camouflage tool

Fig. 147. Design camouflaged

Fig. 148. Holding a shader

Fig. 149. Design shaded

Beveler

This tool, available in several sizes, may be smooth, checked, or lined. Its use makes parts of a design stand out in bold relief. Small bevelers are used in close areas, while large ones are used along straight cuts and large curves. See impressions 203, C3, and C7 in Fig. 145.

28. Hold the beveler as instructed in step 23 with the thick part of the tool in the knife cut. Move the tool along the cut as you strike it, making a smooth, deep bevel. Taper the bevel as you come to the end of a cut by using less striking force on the tool. See Fig. 150.

29. Your design will determine where to bevel. As a rule, bevel on the outside of curves. Always bevel away from that part of the design which you wish to stand out, such as a flower or a part of the design which overlaps another part.

30. Do not bevel around background areas, since background tools will put this leather down later. See Fig. 151.

Veiner and shell tool

These tools, varying in size and shape, are used to decorate plain surfaces on leaves, stems, and flowers. Barkers and shell tools may be substituted for veiners. See impressions 748, F4, 708, and F13 in Fig. 145.

31. Hold the tool as instructed in step 23 except that it is tilted as shown in Fig. 152. Space the impressions uniformly, turning the tool as you stamp to conform to the contour of the design.

32. Use a shell tool to make a sharp impression at the junction of two petals or leaves. See Figs. 153 and 154.

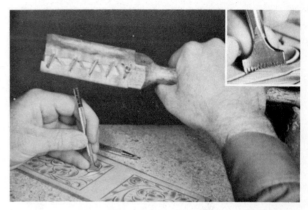

Fig. 152.   Holding a veiner

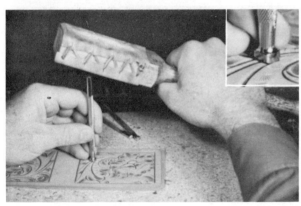

Fig. 150.   Holding a beveler

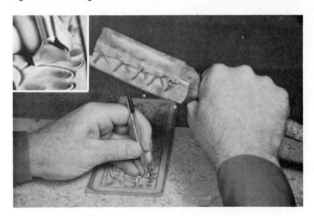

Fig. 153.   Holding a shell tool

Fig. 151   Design beveled

Fig. 154.   Design showing use of veiner and shell tool

Seeders

These tools vary as to design, size, and shape. Their chief use is for flower centers or swirls. See impressions 706, L4, and L7 in Fig. 145.

33. Hold the seeder as instructed in step 23. Do not strike the tool too hard, or you will cut a hole in the leather. Do not overlap the impressions. Stamp the outer circle of seeds first as shown in Fig. 155. Then fill in the remainder of the seed area. See Fig. 156.

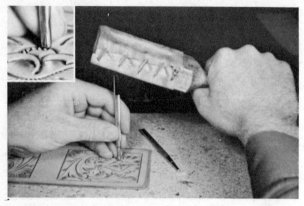

Fig. 155.   Holding a seeder

Fig. 156.   Design showing use of a seeder

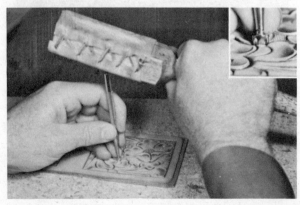

Fig. 157.   Holding a background tool

Background tools

These tools come in several sizes and shapes. See impressions 101, A4, and A7 in Fig. 145. The surface of the leather must be almost dry for good backgrounding.

34. Hold the tool as instructed in step 23. Strike the tool hard enough to make a deep impression, but do not cut through the surface of the leather. See Fig. 157.

35. "Walk" the tool along as you strike it. The impressions should barely touch each other. Clean up the corners by tilting the grounder if the entire surface of the tool is not needed. See Fig. 158.

36. *Never* stamp into the border or design, overlap impressions, leave ragged edges, work on wet leather, or vary the depth of the impressions.

Other saddle stamps

The basic stamps have been discussed and illustrated. It is impossible to show where all of the stamps may be used. With experience and much practice, you will be able to use and adapt many other stamps in decorating a design.

37. After all stamping has been completed, use the broad end of a modeler to smooth or sharpen parts of a design. You might also use a large smooth

Fig. 158.   Design backgrounded

Fig. 159.   Cardboard cemented to leather

shader or beveler for this touch-up work. Remember to use very light pressure and to smooth out only where necessary.

Procedure in carving and stamping lightweight leather

38. After you have conditioned a piece of lightweight leather, but before you cut or stamp it, cement a piece of heavy cardboard to the flesh side. You can obtain deeper impressions without stamping through the leather. The cardboard will also keep the leather from stretching out of shape. See Fig. 159.

39. Cement heavy paper to heavier leathers if they tend to stretch during stamping.

40. Pull the cardboard or paper from the leather after stamping is completed.

Procedure in making ornamental or dress cuts

The last step in carving is to decorate the design with a few well-placed dress cuts.

41. Use a sponge to moisten the grain surface of the leather before you make the cuts. Remember that the leather was almost dry for the background stamping.

42. In starting a dress cut, hold the knife as shown in Fig. 160 with the flat part of the blade parallel to the body. Start the cut deep. Rotate the barrel of the knife rather rapidly between the thumb and fingers as you pull the knife toward your body, making a tapered cut as shown in Fig. 161.

Notice the position of the fingers on the barrel at the start of the cut and at the completion of it. Also notice the angle of the knife at the start and finish of the cut.

43. Practice on prepared scrap leather before attempting to make dress cuts on a project. Make cuts from the right and from the left as shown in Fig. 162. Avoid tails at the ends of dress cuts by carrying the knife straight away from the ends of the tapered cuts.

44. Follow the curvature of the design with the dress cuts as shown in Fig. 163.

45. See Operation 36 for leather finishing.

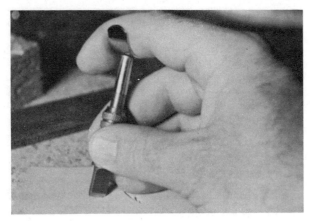

Fig. 160. Starting a dress cut

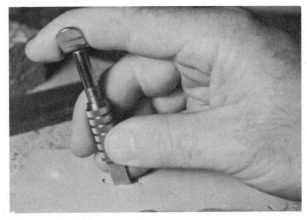

Fig. 161. Completing a dress cut

Fig. 162. Practice dress cuts

Fig. 163. Design with dress cuts

Operation 16   How to use edge tools

Edge tools are used to round, bevel, and finish the edges of leather. They vary in size and shape and are made for either light or heavy leathers. Edge tools with large size numbers are for use on heavy leather.

Procedure

1. For best results, have the leather in the same condition as for tooling. The tools will produce a smoother cut on dampened leather.

2. If the leather is not to be tooled, use the tools on dry leather. There is no need to condition the leather just for this operation.

3. Use the edge beveler to bevel the edges on lightweight leather to prevent fraying. Push it along the edge of the leather, producing a uniform cut. See Fig. 164.

4. Use the common edge tool to bevel or round edges on heavy leather. It may be used on either the grain or flesh side. Push the tool along the edge of the leather, producing a uniform cut. See Fig. 165.

5. The Bissonnette edge tool, which is sometimes called a safety edger, produces a uniform cut and makes a rounded edge on the leather. Push or pull it along the edge. See Fig. 166.

6. Read Operation 36 for information on "How to Finish Edges."

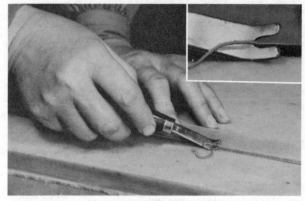
Fig. 165. Using the common edge tool

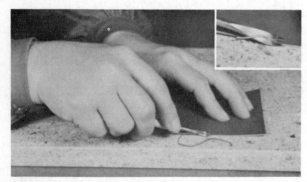
Fig. 164. Using an edge beveler

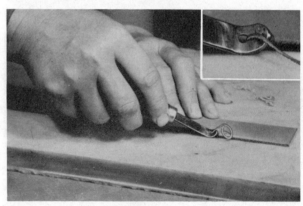
Fig. 166. Using a Bissonnette edge tool

Operation 17   How to use the edge creaser

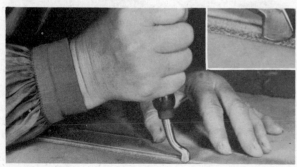
Fig. 167. Using a single edge creaser

Edge creasers come in several sizes. Those with large numbers are for heavy leathers. They are used to crease lines along edges of belts and open edges of pockets. The best edge creaser is a metal one, either single or double.

Procedure

1. Condition the leather as for tooling. (Operation 6.)

2. Bevel raw edges with an edge tool. (Operation 16.)

3. Place the leather upon a flat surface. Push the edge creaser along the edge of the leather, creasing a deep line. Move the tool back and forth until the creased line reaches the desired depth. Use a heavy pressure on the tool. See Fig. 167.

4. Use the edge creaser along a folded edge after the edge has been folded and cemented. (Operations 19 and 35.)

Operation 18   How to skive leather

Skiving is the process of reducing the thickness of leather. It may be the thinning of edges which later will be laced or sewed. Skiving is also done where edges are to fold or the leather is to bend. Reducing the thickness makes the leather more pliable. Various knives may be used for skiving.

Procedure

1. Be sure that your knives are sharp. (Operation 4.)

2. Place the leather upon a flat surface, flesh side up. Use a bevel point knife to skive the leather. Push the knife away from you and make a slicing cut extending ½″ in from the edge and down to one-half the thickness of the leather at the edge as shown in Fig. 168. The depth of the cut will be determined by the number of pieces to be assembled. The assembled edges should equal the original thickness of the leather.

3. Push the bevel-end skiving knife along the edge, cutting the leather as shown in Fig. 169.

4. The head knife is an excellent skiving knife. Hold it as shown in Fig. 170, pushing it along the edge of the leather.

5. The Skife, which is a patented skiving knife, will thin the edges of leather uniformly. Start the skiving at one end as shown in Fig. 171. Pull the Skife toward you. Reverse the leather or your position at the table, and continue to skive in the

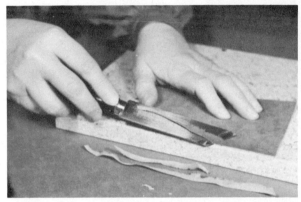

Fig. 169.   Using a bevel-end skiving knife

Fig. 170.   Skiving with a head knife

Fig. 168.   Skiving with a bevel point knife

Fig. 171.   Starting to skive with the Skife

opposite direction as shown in Fig. 172. Practice on scrap leather. A Schick injector razor blade is used in the Skife. It is a very good knife for skiving lace for splicing.

Fig. 172.   Skiving with the Skife

6. Clamp very heavy leather to a table. Skive it with a spokeshave as shown in Fig. 173.

7. *Remember* to keep hands back of all cutting edges.

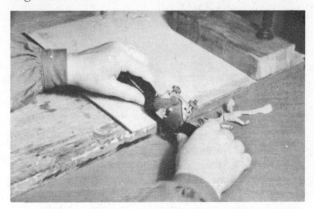

Fig. 173.   Skiving with a spokeshave

Operation 19   How to make folded edges

Open edges of pockets are generally folded to produce a stronger and more finished edge.

Procedure

1. Skive the leather where it must fold. (Operation 18.)

2. Moisten the leather slightly on the flesh side where the fold is to be made.

3. Using the small end of a molder and a straightedge, crease a line on the flesh side along the edge of the pocket where the fold is to be made. This will aid in making the fold. The distance of the crease in from the edge should be ¼" or more, depending upon the allowance made for the fold.

4. Apply cement on the flesh side where the fold will be. See Fig. 174.

5. Fold the leather over. Smooth it down with the fingers. See Fig. 174.

6. Tap the folded edge lightly with a smooth

Fig. 174.   Smoothing down a folded edge

hammer.

7. You may either crease this folded edge with an edge creaser or sew it. Be sure to work on the front or grain side of the leather.

Operation 20   How to fold heavy leather

It is difficult to fold heavy leather to make sharp corners in purse, box, and case construction. Follow the instructions for making folds. Practice on scrap leather.

Procedure

1. Use a scratch awl and straightedge to locate the fold on the flesh side of the leather.

2. Adjust a rampart gouger to cut a groove not

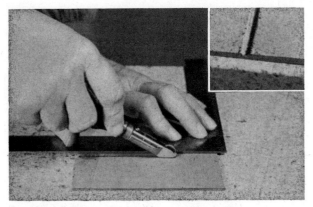

Fig. 175. Cutting a groove with a rampart gouger

Fig. 176. Cutting a V-groove with a knife

more than half the thickness of the leather. Test the depth of the cut on scrap leather.

3. Cut a groove by pushing the gouger along a straightedge as shown in Fig. 175. The insert shows the shape of cut made by this tool.

4. If a gouger is not available, the groove may be cut with a knife. Lay out the line of the fold as in step 1 above. Then lay out lines 1/16″ from this fold line, one on each side.

5. Holding a knife at a 45-degree angle to the leather, cut along the two outside lines laid out in step 4 to a depth of one-half the thickness of the leather. Do not cut too deep. Practice on scrap leather. See Fig. 176. The insert shows the 90-degree groove.

6. Moisten the leather on the flesh side along the groove.

7. Fold the leather to the desired angle.

8. If the leather is very strong and firm, it may be necessary to use a smooth hammer or mallet to stretch and set the leather. Place the leather upon a firm surface. Strike the folded edge lightly

Fig. 177. Setting folded leather

as shown in Fig. 177. Be sure that the leather is moistened properly at the fold or the grain side may crack.

9. After stretching the leather at the fold, set the leather at the desired angle. Let it dry in this position. See the insert in Fig. 177.

10. Always gouge out the leather on the flesh side regardless of which way it is to fold.

Operation 21   How to stretch and form leather

Leather may be stretched and formed to make nose pieces for camera cases. Forming may be necessary in making other projects. The procedure given is general, but the instruction applies to all work of this nature.

Procedure

1. Determine the size and shape of the formed piece.

2. Construct a forming die from white pine. Round all forming edges slightly and sand them

Fig. 178. A forming die for leather

Fig. 179. Leather fastened to a forming die

Fig. 180. Using a clamp on a forming die

very smooth. See Fig. 178. Make the necessary allowance between A and B for the thickness of the leather. See the insert in Fig. 178. B will be the inside dimension of the formed piece.

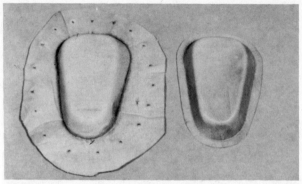

Fig. 181. Formed nose pieces for a camera case

3. Cut 4-oz. cowhide at least 1″ larger than the formed piece. You may experiment with various weights of leather.

4. Case the leather. (Operation 6.)

5. Place the leather over the opening in the die with the grain side down. Fasten the leather to the female part of the die A with small nails around the edge of the leather. Place the male part of the die B over the leather and the opening in the bottom piece of wood. See Fig. 179.

6. Apply pressure to B, forcing it down into the opening of part A. There are several methods of performing this operation. In Fig. 180, small pieces of wood were placed on both sides of the die, and then a clamp was used to force B into A. You might also use a vise or a drill press spindle and drill table for this operation.

7. Let the leather dry in the forming die.

8. After the leather has dried, remove it from the die. Lay out the correct width of the flanged edge with saddler's compasses.

9. Trim off the surplus edge. Fig. 181 shows leather just removed from a die and also a piece on which the edges have been trimmed.

10. Line the formed piece with thin leather if you desire. You might also use flocking if it is available.

Operation 22   How to splice lace

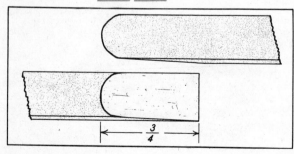

Fig. 182. Splicing a lace

When you lace a project, do not use too long a thong or lace, for it will stretch as it is pulled through the thong slits. A piece of lace about one yard long is a convenient length to use. Since most projects require more than one yard of lace, it is necessary to know how to make a good splice in the lace.

Procedure

1. Skive the end of the used piece of lace on the grain side back ¾″ from the end. Skive the new

length of lace back ¾″ on the flesh side. (Operation 18.)

2. Apply a thin coat of cement to both skived ends. Let it set for a few minutes.

3. Press the ends firmly together. Tap the splice lightly with the end of a tool handle.

4. Be sure that the splice is no thicker than the original thickness of the lace. See Fig. 182.

Operation 23   How to make thong slits

Thong slits made with a thonging chisel will fit up closely around the lacing when it is completed. If the edge to be laced is quite thick, a thonging chisel will tend to cut or break the leather between the slits. For thick edges, round holes should be punched. Instruction for punching round holes is given in Operation 30.

Procedure

1. If possible, skive, cement, and assemble all edges before thonging is done. Round all corners. Use a small coin such as a dime to aid in rounding off a corner. It may not be possible to assemble some projects before thonging the edges.

2. For ³⁄₃₂″ lace, set the patent leather compasses to mark a light line ⅛″ in from the edge of the project as shown in Fig. 183. Be careful not to break through the surface of the leather with the point of the compasses. You may also use an awl and a straightedge to lay out this line. The thong slits may be as far as ¼″ from the edge on large projects where ⅛″ lace is used.

3. Place the project upon a smooth board with the cover up. Select a four-prong thonging chisel of the correct size. Hold it vertically. Tap it with a mallet, using just enough force to cut through the leather. See Fig. 184.

4. Place one prong of the thonging chisel in the last slit cut in order to space the slits evenly. Con-

Fig. 184. Using a four-prong thonging chisel

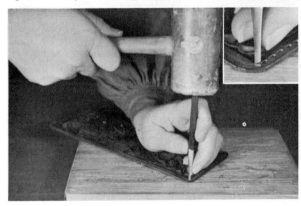
Fig. 185. Using a one-prong chisel

Fig. 183. Using the patent leather compasses

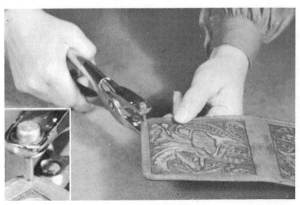
Fig. 186. Using a combination punch at a corner

tinue cutting until a corner is reached. See the insert in Fig. 184.

5. Use a one-prong thonging chisel for cutting the slits at corners or along sharply curved edges. Space the thong slits by placing the chisel upon the leather next to the last slit cut and then moving it over the width of the chisel. See the insert in Fig. 185. Hold the chisel vertically. Strike it with a mallet.

6. You may use a combination punch or universal pliers with the desired size of slitting punch to make the slits at corners. The slits are spaced as in step 5. See Fig. 186.

7. Stop cutting the slits a short distance from the starting point. The last few slits may need different spacing to end properly. Make them slightly closer or farther apart. The slight variation will not be noticed. Cut them with a one-prong chisel.

Operation 24   How to lace with the whipstitch

There are several styles of lacing. The three most common are the whipstitch, single buttonhole stitch, and double buttonhole stitch. The whipstitch is the simplest and requires a length of lace about three times the distance to be laced. Fig. 187 shows the whipstitch.

Procedure

1. Cut the thong slits or punch round holes. (Operation 23 or 30.)

2. Cut off one yard of lace. Start to lace at any convenient place where you can get between the cover and the lining. Working from the back of the project, put a ½″ end of lace through the first thong slit or punched hole in the lining and down between the lining and cover as shown in the cutout window at A, Fig. 188. Cement this end

in place so that the grain side of the lace will be up when it is brought over the edge to the front of the cover. *Do not cut this window in your project.* The opening was cut to show you how the lace is fastened between the lining and the cover.

3. Skive about ⅜″ of the other end of the lace on the flesh side. Fasten this end in a two-point lacing needle. See Fig. 189. There are several types of lacing needles. The two-point needle is preferred by most leathercraft workers. A thin strip of metal may be folded, the lace inserted between the ends, and the metal pointed right at the fold to make a lacing needle.

4. Holding the project with the cover toward you, bring the lace over and insert the needle into the second hole. Pull the lace through until it is tight. Fig. 188, B, shows the needle in the third hole.

5. Lace from left to right, keeping the same slant and tension on the lacing.

6. Splice the lace whenever it is necessary. (Operation 22.)

7. Use an awl to open up the thong slits if they are too tight for the needle.

Fig. 187. The whipstitch

Fig. 188. Starting the whipstitch

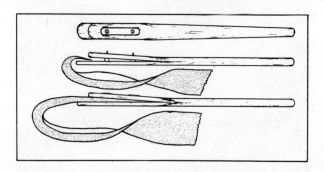

Fig. 189. Fastening lace in a needle

8. In lacing around corners, go twice through two of the holes or thong slits as at C, Fig. 190.

9. Finish the lacing by inserting the lace through the first hole in the cover and then down between the cover and lining as shown at D, Fig. 190. Pull the lace tight. Cut off the surplus. The small window at E, Fig. 190, shows the starting and finishing ends of the lace cemented between the lining and the cover. *Do not cut this window in your project.*

10. If only a single thickness of leather is to be laced, thread the ends of the lace under several stitches on the back of the project.

11. Tap the laced edge. Read step 15, Operation 26.

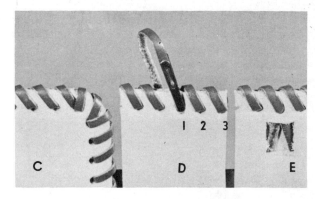

Fig. 190. Completing the whipstitch

Operation 25   How to lace with the single buttonhole stitch

The single buttonhole stitch covers the edges of the leather much better than the whipstitch. The length of lace required is about five times the distance to be laced. This stitch is shown in Fig. 191.

Procedure

1. Cut the thong slits. (Operation 23.) If the edge to be laced is thick, punch round holes. (Operation 30.)

2. Fasten a lacing needle to one end of the lace. (See step 3, Operation 24.)

3. Hold the project with the cover toward you. Start lacing at a point where the ends of the lace may be pulled between the lining and cover at the finish. Insert the needle through the first thong slit or hole. Pull all of the lace through except two inches.

4. Loop the lace around the 2″ end as shown at A, Fig. 192. Then insert the lace through the second hole and tighten it as shown at B, Fig. 192. Remember that the grain side of both the lace and cover should be toward you. Lace from left to right.

5. Next, bring the lace over and under one loop as shown at C, Fig. 192.

6. Hold the leather as shown in Fig. 197 with the first finger back of the entire stitch. Pull the

lace, tightening the stitch. It helps to tighten the stitch if the thumb of the left hand is placed over the stitch and pulled down toward the hole as the lace is tightened.

7. Compare the pictures and your work to see if they are the same. If so, continue to lace.

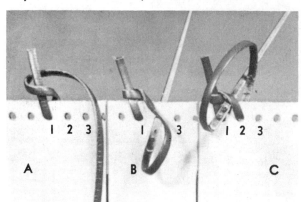

Fig. 192. Steps A B C, single buttonhole stitch

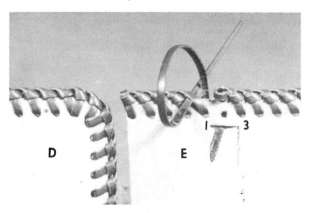

Fig. 193. Steps D E, single buttonhole stitch

Fig. 191. Single buttonhole stitch

8. In lacing around corners, take two stitches in two or more holes as shown at D, Fig. 193, to make a smoothly rounded corner.

9. Splice the lace whenever necessary. (Operation 22.)

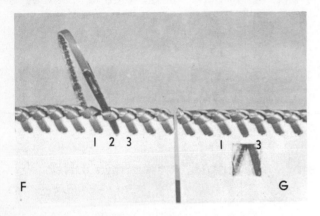

Fig. 194.   Steps F G, single buttonhole stitch

10. Lace around the project to the starting point. Remove the beginning stitches from holes 1 and 2 as shown at E, Fig. 193, since they do not have the same slant as the rest of the lacing. Put the beginning end of the lace through hole 2 from the back and then down between the lining and cover as shown in the window at E, Fig. 193. Cement ½" of this end to the lining. Cut off the surplus.

11. Lace up to the open loop as shown at E, Fig. 193. Tighten the stitch at hole 1. Put the needle through the open loop and down through hole 2 of the cover between the lining and cover as shown at F, Fig. 194.

12. Pull the lace down between the cover and the lining. Tighten the stitch until it looks like G, Fig. 194. Cement ½" of the finishing end of the lace to the lining beside the starting end. The small opening was cut in the cover to show you how the ends of the lace look cemented into place. *Do not cut this opening in your project.*

13. Tap the laced edge. Read step 15, Operation 26.

Operation 26   How to lace with the double buttonhole stitch

The double buttonhole stitch covers the edges of the leather much better than the single buttonhole stitch. This stitch is sometimes called the double

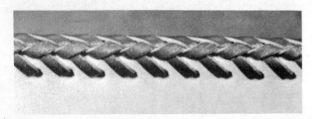

Fig. 195.   Double buttonhole stitch

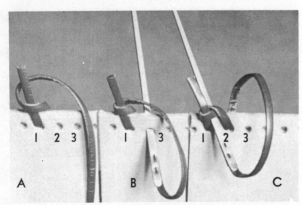

Fig. 196.   Steps A B C, double buttonhole stitch

cordovan or double overlay. See Fig. 195. The length of lace required is about seven times the distance to be laced. Read each step in the procedure carefully and study the pictures.

Procedure

1. Make thong slits or punch round holes. (Operation 23 or 30.)

2. Fasten a lacing needle to one end of the lace. (See step 3, Operation 24.)

3. Hold the project with the cover toward you. Lace from left to right. If possible, start lacing at a point which can be easily reached from the inside of the project and yet will not show the ends of the lace when the lacing is completed.

4. Pull all but about two inches of the lace through the first hole. Make a loop as shown at A, Fig. 196.

5. Hold the 2" loose end down on the back with the first finger of the left hand. Tighten the loop. Insert the lace through the second hole as shown at B, Fig. 196.

6. The lacing up to this point is the same as the single buttonhole stitch. The only difference between the two stitches is that in the double buttonhole stitch the lace is brought over and put under two loops as shown at C, Fig. 196, instead of one as in the single buttonhole stitch.

7. Hold the leather as shown in Fig. 197 with the first finger back of the entire stitch. Pull the lace, tightening the stitch. It helps to tighten the stitch if the thumb of the left hand is placed over the stitch and pulled down toward the hole as the lace is tightened.

8. Start the next stitch by bringing the lace over and inserting it through the third hole. Pull it up snug. The loose end which was held down may now be released. Then put the lace under two loops as shown at D, Fig. 198. Tighten the second stitch.

9. Be sure that the grain side of the lace is toward you and that there are no twists in the lace. Keep the same slant on the lacing. Splice the lace whenever necessary. (Operation 22.) *Does your lacing look like the picture?*

10. Lace around corners as shown at E, Fig. 198. Take two stitches in two or more holes to make a smoothly rounded corner.

11. Lace around the project to the starting point. Remove the two beginning stitches from holes 1 and 2 since they do not have the same slant as the rest of the lacing. Put the beginning end of the lace through hole 2 from the back and then down between the lining and cover as shown in the cutout window at F, Fig. 199. Cement ½″ of this end to the lining. Notice the open loop.

12. Lace up to this open loop and hole 2. Complete the stitch by going through hole 1 as shown at F, Fig. 199, and then inserting the lace up through the open loop from the bottom and then back under the two loops as shown at G, Fig. 199.

13. Next, bring the lace over and down through the loop and hole 2 of the cover and then down between the cover and the lining as shown at H, Fig. 200.

14. Pull the lace between the cover and lining. Tighten the stitch until it looks like I, Fig. 200.

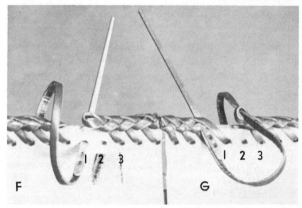

Fig. 199. Steps F G, double buttonhole stitch

Fig. 197. Correct way to hold leather during lacing

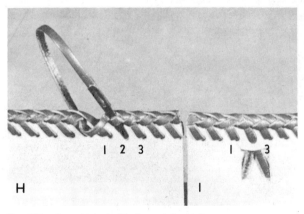

Fig. 200. Steps H I, double buttonhole stitch

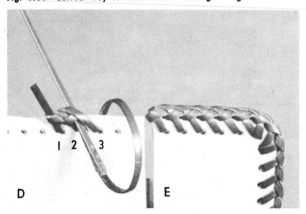

Fig. 198. Steps D E, double buttonhole stitch

Fig. 201. Using a hammer to set a laced edge

Work the stitch between the fingers to get the same slant as on the rest of the lacing. Cement ½″ of the finishing end of the lace to the lining beside the starting end. Cut off the surplus lace. The opening at I, Fig. 200, was cut merely to show you how the two ends of lace look between the layers of leather. *Do not cut this opening in your project.*

15. Use a smooth mallet or hammer to flatten the laced edge. See Fig. 201. Place the under side of the laced edge upon a piece of marble. Tap the edge lightly on the finished side with a hammer or mallet.

Operation 27   How to do Florentine lacing

Florentine or Venetian lace is often used to lace the edges of book covers, albums, desk pads, and picture frames. Florentine lace, which is generally cut from kidskin, is very soft and pliable. The amount of lace needed is about three times the distance to be laced.

Procedure

1. You can buy Florentine lace in either ¼″ or ⅜″ widths. You may also cut it from a skin with scissors or a knife.

2. Lay out and punch holes for the lace. Use a No. 0 punch for ¼″ lace and No. 1 for ⅜″ lace. Space the holes the width of the lace. The distance of the holes from the edge will vary up to 5⁄16″.

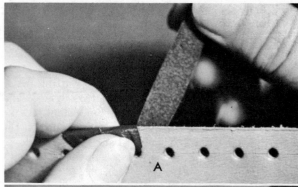

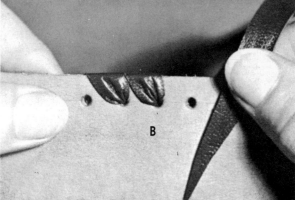

Fig. 203. Finishing a Florentine stitch

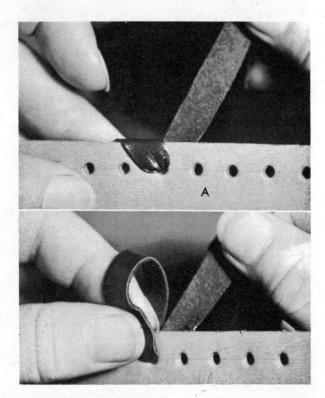

Fig. 202. Starting Florentine lacing

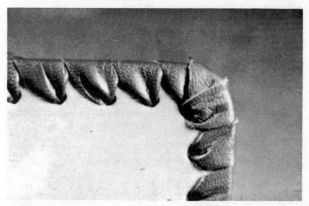

Fig. 204. Lacing around a corner

Practice lacing in scrap leather. Vary the size of the holes and the distance from the edge to determine the best size and distance. (Operation 30.)

3. Point a piece of lace.

4. Hold the project with the cover toward you. Put the lace through the first hole, working from front to back. Pull it through until a 2″ end remains. Bring this loose end over to the back. Hold it down with the second finger of the left hand as shown at A, Fig. 202.

5. Bring the lace over and pull it through the second hole. To keep the lace from twisting as it is pulled through the holes, let it slide between the thumb and first finger as shown at B, Fig. 202.

6. Pull the stitch up tight with the thumb over the lace. Apply pressure toward the edge of the leather as shown at A, Fig. 203.

7. The completed stitch is shown at B, Fig. 203.

8. In lacing around corners, go through each corner hole twice, or even three times if needed, in order to cover the edge of the leather. See Fig. 204.

9. To finish the lacing, point the loose end of the lace. Run both ends of the lace under two stitches on the back. Cut off the surplus lace.

Operation 28   How to do hand sewing

It is important to know how to do hand sewing. It is almost impossible to sew the hard-to-get-at corners and very heavy leather on a standard sewing machine. Hand sewing is superior to machine sewing in most cases. The stitches can be pulled tighter and will not loosen so easily as the machine-made lock stitch.

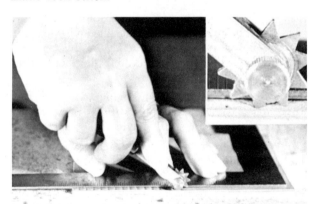

Fig. 205. Using a space marker with a straightedge

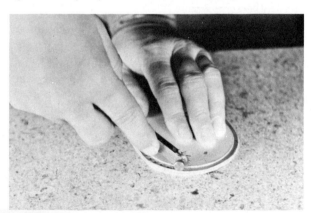

Fig. 206. Using a space marker with a template

Practice hand sewing on scrap leather before sewing on a project.

Procedure for laying out and punching stitch holes
lightweight leather

1. Cement the edges to be sewed together to keep them from slipping.

2. Draw or crease a very light line on the grain side, approximately 1/16″ from the edge of the work. This will mark the location of the stitching holes. The type of construction will help to determine the exact location of the stitching line.

3. Determine how many stitches are to be made per inch. On small projects and lightweight leather, there should be from eight to twelve stitches. If twelve or more stitches are to be made, you must use a very small needle and fine thread. There is

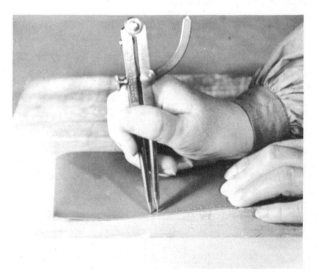

Fig. 207. Using dividers to punch stitch holes

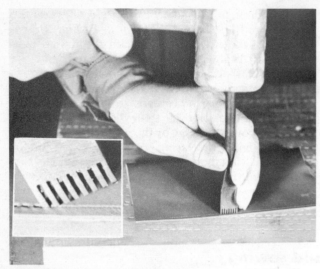

Fig. 208. Using a stitching punch

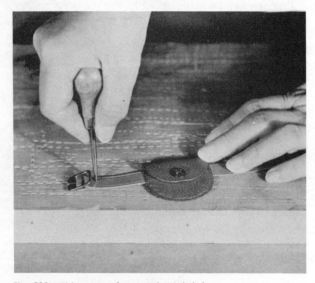

Fig. 209. Using an awl to punch stitch holes

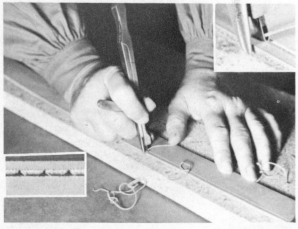

Fig. 210. Cutting a groove for stitching

a tendency to cut the leather between stitches if too fine a stitch is used.

4. Use the correct space marker to mark the stitch holes. For straight lines, use a straightedge as a guide. See Fig. 205. For curves, use a cardboard template. See Fig. 206.

5. Use dividers to mark and punch the stitch holes if a space marker is not available. Set the dividers for the length of stitch desired. Step off and punch the stitch holes as shown in Fig. 207.

6. Use a stitching punch to cut stitch holes in very lightweight leather. Place the leather upon a smooth board. Hold the punch vertically. Strike it with a mallet, cutting just through the leather. Place one prong of the punch in the last hole cut in order to keep the spacing even. See Fig. 208. Do *not* use a space marker if you use a stitching punch.

7. Use an awl to punch stitch holes in lightweight leather. Place the leather upon a smooth board. Force the awl through the leather by hand. See Fig. 209.

heavy leather

8. If possible, cement the edges to be sewed together.

9. Lay out a line to mark the distance from the edge for the stitching line. This line will vary up to ¼″ for heavy leather. Here again the type of construction will help to determine the location of the stitching line.

10. Use a space marker or dividers to mark the stitch holes. Use four to seven stitches per inch on heavy leather. Read steps 4 and 5.

11. If the stitches will receive heavy wear, as in sandal soles, cut a groove for the thread with patent leather compasses.

12. Fasten one of the scratches to the compasses. Adjust the compasses. Cut the groove as shown in Fig. 210. Damp leather will cut more easily than dry leather.

13. Mark the stitching holes in the bottom of the groove. See the insert in Fig. 210.

14. If possible, use a stitching horse to hold heavy leather for sewing. It is an ideal way. See Fig. 211. You may also hold the leather in a jaw-clamp or between two boards held in a vise as shown in Fig. 212.

15. Use a saddler's haft and awl to punch a hole at each stitch mark as shown in Fig. 213. Hold the wide part of the awl at an angle of 45 degrees to the edge of the leather. See the insert for the shape of the punched holes. Punch a few holes at a time, just ahead of the sewing.

16. You may drill stitch holes in very heavy leather. Lay out the stitch holes. Use a 1/16" drill for a No. 000 harness needle. The insert in Fig. 214 shows sewing done in drilled holes. The drill must be the size of the needle. A large hole will weaken the leather and the stitching.

Procedure for sewing
lightweight leather

17. Select the correct needle and the weight and kind of thread for lightweight leather. Read the information on needles and threads on pages 18 and 19.

18. You need not punch stitch holes in very lightweight leather if you use a glover's needle.

19. A running stitch is a good stitch for beginners to use on lightweight leather. Sew in one direction. Start down through the leather as shown at 1, Fig. 215, then up through the leather as shown at 2, down through the leather as at 3, and so on to the end of the sewing. Then sew back, filling in the alternate stitches as shown in Fig. 215. Pull each stitch tight, but do not cut the leather. Tie the ends of the thread after the sewing is completed. Cut off the surplus thread. Place a small amount of cement on the knot. Tap it lightly with a hammer.

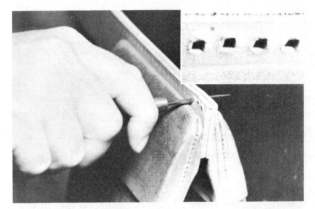

Fig. 213.   Using a saddler's haft and awl

Fig. 211.   A stitching horse

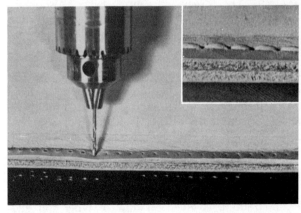

Fig. 214.   Drilling stitch holes

Fig. 212.   Leather held in a vise

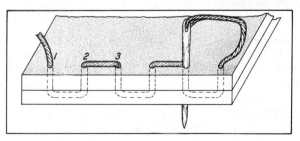

Fig. 215.   Sewing, using the running stitch

Fig. 216.   Burning ends of nylon thread

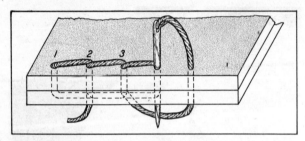

Fig. 217.   Sewing, using the backstitch

each cord and with a quick pull remove some of the fibers. See C in Fig. 218.

24. Pull the thinned ends through some beeswax as shown at D, Fig. 218.

25. Twist the waxed cords into a tapered point as shown at E, Fig. 218.

making waxed thread

26. Determine the strength of thread needed.

27. Cut off the number of strands of No. 10 Barbour's flax thread needed for thread of the desired strength. Do not make these strands more than six feet in length.

20. To keep the tied ends of nylon thread from coming untied, leave about ½″ ends on the thread at the knot. Burn these ends with a match. See Fig. 216. The thread will burn easily. As soon as the ends burn down to the knot, press the knot firmly with a finger. The knot will be fused together. See the insert in Fig. 216.

21. Use the backstitch where only the outside of the project is to show. Start the stitch up through hole 2, then down through 1, next up through 3, down through 2, up through 4, down through 3, and so on until the sewing is completed. See Fig. 217. Fasten the thread securely on the under side at both the beginning and end of the sewing.

heavy leather

The saddler's stitch is used in sewing heavy leather. Instruction is given on how to taper the end of flax thread, how to make waxed thread, and how to fasten waxed thread to a needle, as well as how to do the actual sewing.

tapering flax thread

22. Untwist 2″ of the cords at the end of a heavy flax thread. Fig. 218, A, shows a 7-cord thread.

23. Thin the ends of the cords by pulling the untwisted thread under the edge of a knife held at a right angle to the thread. See B in Fig. 218. An alternate way to thin the ends is to untwist

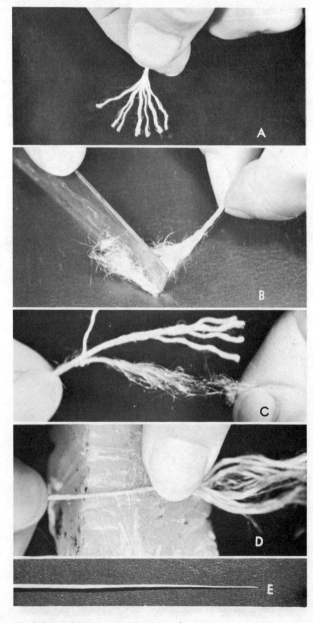

Fig. 218.   Making a tapered point on thread

28. To make a 4-cord thread, taper one end of each of the four strands as given in steps 23, 24, and 25.

29. Place the four tapered ends not more than ½″ apart as shown at A, Fig. 219. Pull the four strands through some beeswax as shown at B, Fig. 219. Fasten the untapered ends of the strands in a vise. Holding the other ends taut, rub them vigorously with a piece of canvas. The heat generated makes the wax penetrate the fibers.

30. Remove the strands from the vise. Roll the waxed strands with the palm of your right hand on your knee or a flat surface as shown at C, Fig. 219. Start with the tapered ends. Be sure to roll the four strands in the direction opposite from that in which they were twisted in the making of the No. 10 thread.

31. Roll about three or four inches of the thread at a time. To prevent kinking of the four strands keep a slight tension on them with the left hand as you roll them with the right. After rolling the cords into a thread, apply more wax. Rub the thread vigorously with the canvas. The 4-cord thread and tapered end are shown at D, Fig. 219.

fastening waxed thread to a needle

32. Put 3″ of the tapered end of the thread through the eye of a harness needle as shown at A, Fig. 220.

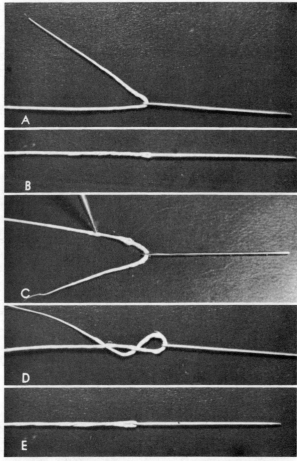

Fig. 220. Fastening waxed thread to a needle

33. If the end is well waxed, you can roll it into the thread back of the eye of the needle. See B, Fig. 220.

34. For a more permanent fastening, use an awl to open up the cords of the thread back about ½″ and 1″ from the eye of the needle as shown at C, Fig. 220.

35. Run the tapered end of the thread through these openings as shown at D, Fig. 220. Pull the thread up tight and wax it. Roll the end so that the thread will look as shown at E, Fig. 220.

saddler's stitch

36. Mark the stitch holes. See step 4. Fasten the leather in the jaws of a stitching horse or vise.

37. Punch holes as given in step 15.

38. Fasten each end of the thread to a harness needle.

39. Pass one needle through the first hole as shown in Fig. 221. Pull the thread through the hole until an equal length of thread is on each side of the leather.

40. Pass both needles through the second hole at the same time but in opposite directions. Be care-

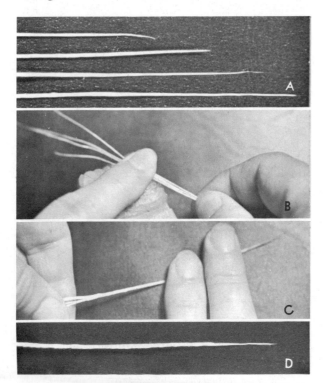

Fig. 219. Making a 4-cord thread

ful not to split the thread. If both needles will not pass freely, pass only one needle through the hole at a time. See Fig. 222.

41. Pull the thread through from both sides until it is snug. Tighten each stitch by pulling the thread from both sides at the same time as shown in Fig. 223. Sew toward you. Punch holes as necessary. The insert in Fig. 223 shows a cross section of the stitch.

42. Finish sewing by going back into two stitches as shown at A, Fig. 224. Cut off the surplus

thread close to the leather as shown at B, Fig. 224.

43. Tap the stitching lightly with a smooth-faced hammer.

44. If a groove was cut in the leather as given in steps 11 and 12, do the sewing as given in the preceding steps. The only difference is that the sewing will be recessed.

45. When there is danger of the saddler's stitch loosening, it may be locked. As you pull the stitch up tight, leave a small loop on the right side. Put

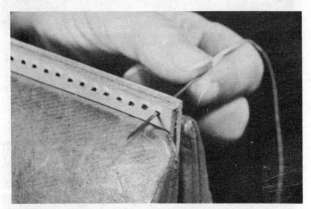

Fig. 221.   Starting the saddler's stitch

Fig. 222.   First stitch in the saddler's stitch

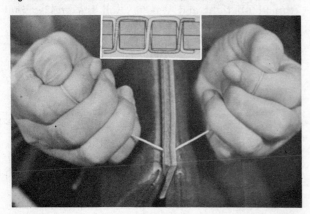

Fig. 223.   Tightening the saddler's stitch

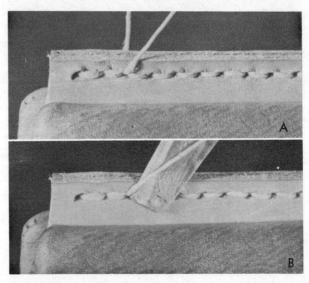

Fig. 224.   Finishing the saddler's stitch

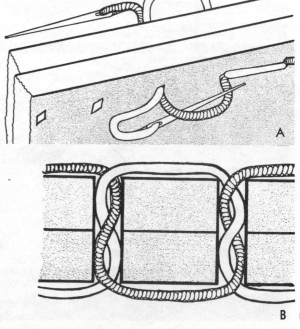

Fig. 225.   A locked saddler's stitch

the needle and thread through this loop as shown at A, Fig. 225. Pull the thread up tight on both sides. Fig. 225, B, shows a cross section of the stitch.

46. In very thick leather, the stitch may be locked so that it is almost impossible to remove it. Leave two loops instead of one as in step 45. Put the needles and thread through these loops as shown at A, Fig. 226. Tighten the stitch. Fig. 226, B, shows a cross section of this stitch.

lock stitch sewing awl

This type of sewing awl is excellent for repair work. See Fig. 39. Specific directions come with the awl when you buy it. The instruction given here is only general.

47. Mark the spaces for the stitches.

48. Wind thread on the reel of the sewing awl.

49. Put the thread through the eye of the needle so that the thread is in the groove of the needle and the end of the thread extends at least 1″ beyond the point of the needle.

50. Hold the awl as shown in Fig. 227 with the long groove of the needle down. Push the needle through the leather about ⅝″.

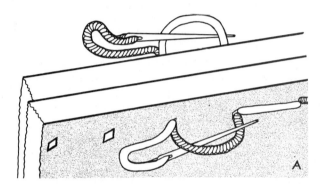

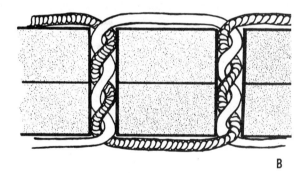

Fig. 226. A double-locked saddler's stitch

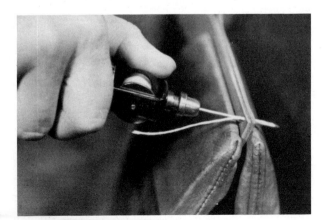

Fig. 227. Holding a sewing awl

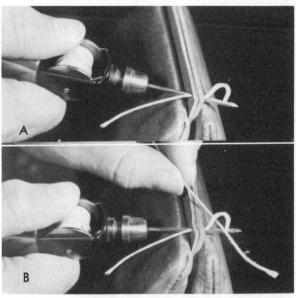

Fig. 228. Starting the lock stitch

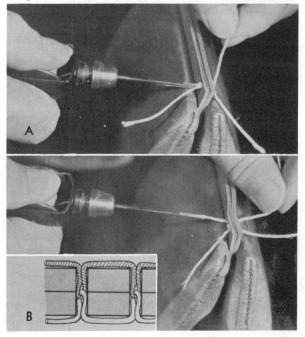

Fig. 229. Completing the lock stitch

51. Pull the needle back through the leather until a loop forms in the thread at the point of the needle. See A, Fig. 228.

52. Put a second piece of thread through this loop. See B, Fig. 228.

53. Use your thumb to keep the reel of thread from turning. Pull the needle the rest of the way back through the leather. See A, Fig. 229.

54. Tighten the stitch by pulling the thread on the left side and pulling the awl with the thread on the right side at the same time. See B and C, Fig. 229.

55. Regulate the tension on the thread by the pressure of your thumb on the reel. Repeat steps 50 through 54 for the next stitch. Continue until the sewing is completed.

Operation 29   How to sew leather by machine

Most sewing machines found in the home can be used to sew medium-weight leather. It is not advisable to use a small portable electric machine unless the leather is very thin. Machine sewing is best for sewing zippers to leather and pockets to linings.

Procedure

1. If you do not know how to use the sewing machine, obtain instruction on your particular machine from the sewing machine company.

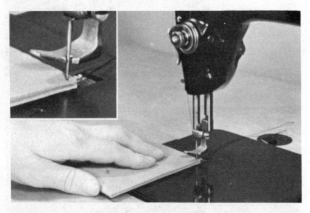

Fig. 230. Starting the first stitch on a machine

2. Cement together the edges of the pieces to be sewed. This keeps them from slipping. Always cement zippers into place before sewing them. (Operation 35.)

3. Use a No. C machine-twist nylon thread for very lightweight leather and No. E for medium-weight leather.

4. Always use the same kind of thread in the bobbin as in the needle.

5. Set the stitch-regulating lever or screw so that the machine will sew from 5 to 8 stitches per inch for heavy leather and from 8 to 12 stitches per inch for lightweight leather. With heavy thread and a large needle, too many stitches per inch will cut the leather. Practice sewing on scrap leather of the same weight as that to be sewed. Check the tension to see that the stitch is locked within the leather and not on the under side.

6. Start sewing by laying both ends of the thread back under the pressure foot. Place the leather just far enough under the pressure foot that the needle when brought down will pierce the leather about a stitch length from the edge as shown in Fig. 230. Lower the pressure foot and begin sewing.

7. In completing the sewing, stop the machine

Fig. 231. Reversing work on the sewing machine

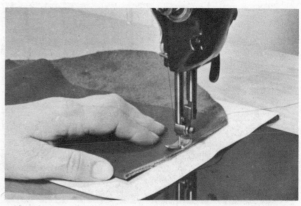

Fig. 232. Protecting leather with paper

at the last stitch with the needle down. Raise the pressure foot and reverse the leather. The needle serves as a pivot. See Fig. 231. Lower the pressure foot and sew back four stitches. Be sure that the needle goes back into the original stitch holes.

8. Cut off the ends of the thread flush with the leather. You may leave longer ends on the thread, pull the top thread through to the under side, and tie the ends together. Read step 20 in Operation 28.

9. If the feed dog marks the leather, place a piece of paper between the leather and the feed dog. See Fig. 232. Tear the paper away after the sewing has been completed.

10. Tap all sewing lightly with a smooth-faced hammer.

Operation **30**   How to use punches

Punches are to cut round, oval, or oblong holes in leather and to shape the ends of straps. The most common punch is the 6-tube revolving type. All types of punches come in several sizes. Some of the punch sizes and the sizes of the holes cut are given in Fig. 233. The sizes of the punches may vary slightly according to the manufacturer.

Procedure for revolving and round drive punches

1. Lay out on the leather the exact location of the hole to be punched. Mark it with an awl.

2. If you are not sure of the size of the hole, punch a hole in scrap leather to check the size.

3. Center the correct tube of the revolving punch directly over the mark. See Fig. 234. Punch the hole.

4. Use a drive punch for places where a revolving punch will not reach because of the shallow throat of the tool. Place the leather upon a piece of wood. Hold the punch vertically and strike it with a mallet. See Fig. 235. *Never* use a hammer on punches.

5. If a drive punch is not available, use the revolving punch as a drive punch. Select the tube desired. Place it opposite the anvil. Close the punch. Place the tube where the hole is to be punched. Strike the punch over the anvil with a mallet. See Fig. 236.

Punch No. 00.....3/64″	Punch No. 4 .....1/8″
Punch No. 0 .....1/16″	Punch No. 5 .....9/64″
Punch No. 1 .....5/64″	Punch No. 6 .....5/32″
Punch No. 2 .....3/32″	Punch No. 7 .....3/16″
Punch No. 3 .....7/64″	Punch No. 8 .....1/4″

Fig. 233.   Punch sizes

Fig. 235.   Using a drive punch

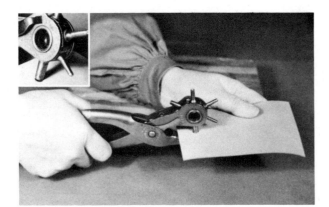

Fig. 234.   Using a revolving punch

Fig. 236.   Using a revolving punch as a drive punch

6. If a hole is to be punched deep in a purse pocket, place a piece of heavy scrap leather in the pocket. Use a drive punch to punch the hole, cutting into the scrap leather. Be careful not to cut through the scrap leather.

Procedure for bag or oblong punches

These punches vary in size from ¼" to 2". They are used to punch holes in gussets for bag straps and openings in straps for belt buckles.

7. Lay out the opening on the leather.

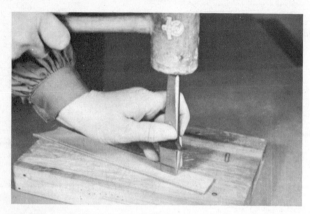

Fig. 237.   Using an oblong punch

Fig. 238.   Using an English-point punch

8. Place the leather upon a piece of wood. Center the oblong punch. Be sure to hold the punch vertically as you strike it with a mallet. See Fig. 237.

Procedure for strap end punches

These punches also vary in size from ¼" to 2". Two styles are available, a half-round punch which cuts a full half circle and the English-point punch which cuts a strap end to a point.

9. Place a punch of the desired size upon the end of the strap. Strike it with a mallet. Be sure to hold the punch vertically. Always have the strap on a piece of wood. See Fig. 238.

Procedure for single tube belt punch

This punch with a two-way gauge is used to punch round holes for lacing, spacing them uniformly.

10. Screw the correct size of tube into the punch. Use a No. 00 tube for ³⁄₃₂" lace and a No. 0 for ⅛" lace.

11. As you set and adjust the punch, check it on scrap leather.

12. Set the depth gauge, which is the flat gauge, ⅛" in from the center of the punch for ³⁄₃₂" lace and ⅛" to ¼" for ⅛" lace. Turn the spacing gauge, which is the pointed gauge, out of the way. Punch a hole in scrap leather to test the setting. Be sure that the edge of the leather is against the gauge. See Fig. 239.

13. Punch a second hole ³⁄₁₆" to the right of the first hole for ³⁄₃₂" lace and ¼" for ⅛" lace. Loosen the spacing gauge which is the pointed gauge. Insert it into the first hole. Close the punch so that the tube is back in the second hole. Set the point of the gauge against the right side of the first hole. Tighten the gauge. See Fig. 240.

14. Punch a third hole, testing the setting of the gauges. Always have the depth gauge against the edge of the leather and the spacing gauge against the right side of the preceding hole.

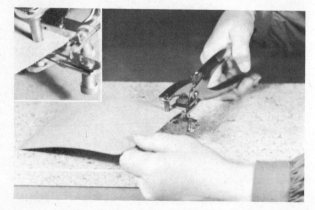

Fig. 239.   Setting the depth gauge on a punch

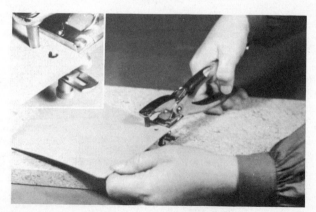

Fig. 240.   Setting the spacing gauge on a punch

15. If the setting is correct, tighten both gauges. Continue punching holes, working from left to right. Check from time to time to see that the gauges have not loosened.

16. If the attachment gauges are not available and round holes are needed for lacing, lay out the holes. Measure in from the edge of the leather the desired distance. Draw a light line with a pencil or an awl. Set a pair of dividers for the distance desired between holes. Step off the distance. Center the tube of the punch over each mark made by the dividers. Punch the holes.

Operation 31   How to set eyelets and grommets

Eyelets are used to fasten frames or metal plates to leather and to reinforce holes in belts. Size No. 00 is large, while No. 3 is small. The No. 1 eyelet is the most common one for leathercraft.

Grommets are considered as eyelets with washers. They are used in awnings, tents, drawstring purses, and tied snapshot albums. The sizes range from No. 00-$\frac{3}{16}$″ to No. 6-1$\frac{3}{16}$″. Teeth-grommets are used on fabrics.

Procedure for eyelets

1. Lay out and punch a hole for the eyelet. (Operation 30.) Check the size of the hole in scrap leather.

2. Place the eyelet A upon the bench top, the leather B over the eyelet, and the metal plate C over the leather and the eyelet. See Figs. 241 and 242.

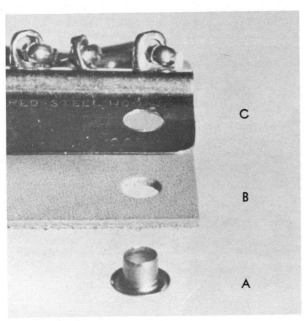

Fig. 241. Steps in inserting an eyelet

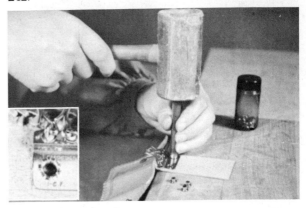

Fig. 243. Setting an eyelet

Fig. 242. Eyelet in place for setting

Fig. 244. Grommet die and grommet

3. Hold the eyelet setter over the eyelet in a vertical position. Strike the tool with a mallet. See Fig. 243. The insert in Fig. 243 shows a set eyelet.

Procedure for grommets

4. Lay out and punch a hole with a grommet cutter or drive punch. (Operation 30.) Holes for

Fig. 245.   Placing leather over a grommet

Fig. 246.   A grommet ready for setting

large grommets are slightly smaller than the grommets. Fig. 244 shows a grommet setting die, a grommet, and a washer.

5. Put a grommet upon a die of the correct size. Place the leather over the grommet, grain side down. Sec Fig. 245.

6. Place the washer, convex side up, over the grommet and the leather. Place the tapered point of the punch into the grommet and die. See Fig. 246.

7. Be sure to hold the punch vertically. Strike it two or three sharp blows with a mallet. See Fig. 247. The insert in Fig. 247 shows the grommet and the washer side of the grommet.

8. If the hole in the leather is too small for the leather to go over the grommet easily, place the leather over the grommet, the washer over the hole in the leather, and then insert the punch. Strike the punch, thus forcing the grommet through the hole.

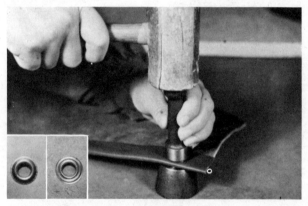

Fig. 247.   Setting a grommet

Operation 32   How to set rivets and spots

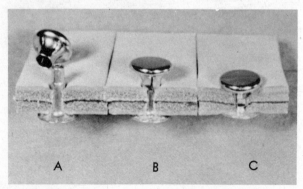

Fig. 248.   Steps in setting a rivet

Rapid rivets are available in several lengths for different thicknesses of leather. They are used for permanent construction. Ornamental spots come in various sizes and shapes. They may be solid metal or jeweled spots. They are used to decorate belts, dog harness, holsters, etc.

Procedure for rapid rivets

1. Locate and punch a hole for the base of the rivet.

2. Insert the base of the rivet into the hole as shown at A, Fig. 248.

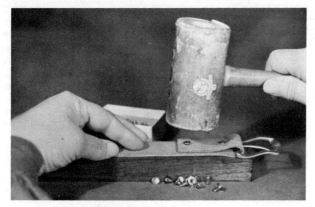

Fig. 249. Setting a rapid rivet

Fig. 250. Using a hand tool to cut slits

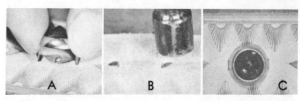

Fig. 251. Fastening a spot into place

3. Place the top of the rivet over the base as shown at B, Fig. 248.

4. Place the rivet and leather upon a bench. Strike the top of the rivet with a mallet. See Fig. 249. The rivet is shown set at C, Fig. 248.

Procedure for ornamental spots

5. Locate the positions for the spots on the leather.

6. Set the blades on the hand tool for the distance between the prongs on a spot. Cut the slits for the prongs as shown in Fig. 250. Be sure that the leather is on a board.

7. If a hand tool is not available, use a one-prong thonging chisel to cut the slits.

8. Push the prongs of the spot through the slits from the grain side of the leather as shown at A, Fig. 251. Be sure that the jewel is in the frame

on all two-part spots.

9. Bend the prongs back on the flesh side as shown at B, Fig. 251. The spot is shown fastened into place at C, Fig. 251.

10. If a great many spots are to be set, drill a shallow hole, slightly smaller than the frame of the spot, in a piece of wood. Place the spot into this hole. Bend the prongs down against the flesh side of the leather with a mallet.

Operation 33 — How to set snap fasteners

Read the information about snap fasteners on page 19.

Procedure for birdcage snap buttons

1. Check the four parts of a birdcage snap button as shown in Fig. 252. The cap and eyelet form one unit, the spring and post the other.

2. Locate and punch a hole the correct size for the eyelet. (Operation 30.) Test the hole for size in scrap leather.

3. Place the eyelet over the anvil of the snap attaching set. Push the leather down over the eyelet, grain side up. Then put the cap over the eyelet. See Fig. 253.

4. If you cannot press the eyelet into the hole easily, use the bodkin F, as shown in Fig. 253.

5. Place the concave part of the hammer of the snap attaching set on top of the cap. Strike the tool with a mallet, thus setting the cap and eyelet. See Fig. 254.

6. Locate the hole for the post by measuring. You may also align all parts and then press the

Cap   Eyelet   Spring   Post

Fig. 252. Parts of a snap button

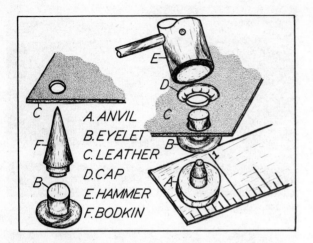

Fig. 253.   Steps in setting the cap and eyelet

Fig. 254.   Setting the cap and eyelet

Fig. 255.   Setting the spring and post

cap firmly. The eyelet will leave an impression on the leather, thus locating the position of the post.

7. Punch a hole for the post.

8. Place the post 2, over the small anvil of the snap attaching set 1; the leather 3, over the post; and the spring 4, over the post and leather. See the insert in Fig. 255.

9. Place the hole in the hammer 5, over the spring. Strike the tool with a mallet, thus setting the spring and post. See Fig. 255.

10. Test the snap button. If it is too loose, tap the spring lightly. If the cap will not close over the spring, compress the spring slightly with a pair of pliers.

11. To set a spring and post deep in a purse pocket, insert the post through the hole from the inside of the pocket. (See step 6, Operation 30, for information about punching the hole.) Put the anvil inside the pocket under the post. Place cloth under the tool and upon the bench top to protect the leather. Place the spring over the post and the tool over the spring. Set the spring and post as shown in Fig. 256.

Procedure for Segma snap fasteners

12. Check the four parts of a Segma snap as shown in Fig. 257. The button and socket form one unit, the eyelet and stud the other.

13. Set the Segma snap the same way as you did the birdcage snap button. You must use the correct size of Segma snap tool for each size of Segma snap.

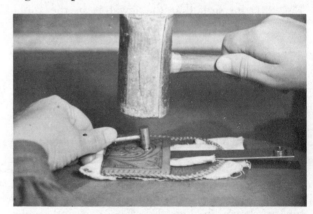

Fig. 256.   Setting a spring and post in a coin purse

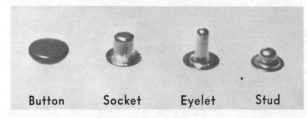

Button   Socket   Eyelet   Stud

Fig. 257.   Parts of a Segma snap

Operation 34   How to attach bag locks

There are two main types of bag locks, the turn lock and the snap lock. The turn lock is most commonly used.

Procedure for turn lock

1. Tool the cover for the purse. Apply a leather finish. (Operation 36.)

2. Fold the cover of the purse to shape. Locate the position of the lock as shown at A, Fig. 258. The size and shape of the lock should harmonize with the design of the purse.

3. Lay out and cut a hole in the flap of the purse the size of the opening in plate 2 shown in Fig. 259. See B, Fig. 258.

4. With the purse again folded to shape, put the prongs of the turn lock, 3 in Fig. 259, through the hole cut in the flap. Press the prongs against the body of the purse, thus marking the leather where slits are to be cut for the prongs. See C, Fig. 258.

5. Cut the slits with a one-prong thonging chisel. (Operation 23.)

6. Insert the prongs of the turn lock through the slits as shown at D, Fig. 258.

7. Place the back plate, 4 in Fig. 259, over the prongs on the flesh side of the leather. Bend the prongs over this plate as shown at E, Fig. 258.

8. Cement the lining to the cover. (Operation 35.) The lining will cover the prongs and the back plate of the turn lock.

9. If you have already lined the purse, then cement a small piece of the lining leather over the prongs.

10. Since the lining also covers the hole in the flap of the purse, B in Fig. 258, cut out the lining to the shape of the hole.

11. Insert the rounded end projections of plate 1, Fig. 259, through the hole in the flap from the grain side. See F, Fig. 258.

12. Place plate 2, Fig. 259, over the end projections on the lining side. Bend the ends down against this plate as shown at G, Fig. 258.

13. See the attached lock at H, Fig. 258.

14. Complete the assembly of the purse.

15. Fig. 260 shows the parts of a turn lock which does not require cutting out the leather. Fold the purse to shape. See A, Fig. 261. Locate the position of the lock loop, 1 in Fig. 260, on the edge of the flap as shown at B, Fig. 261. Do not clamp it to the leather.

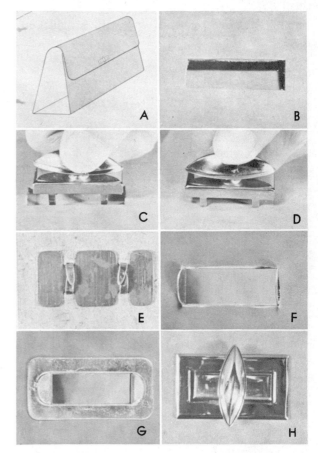

Fig. 258. Attaching a turn lock

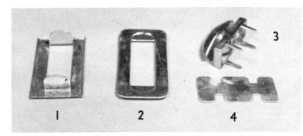

Fig. 259. Parts of a turn lock

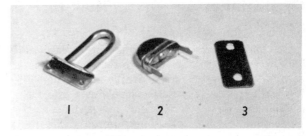

Fig. 260. Parts of an alternate turn lock

16. Place the turn lock, 2 in Fig. 260, into part 1, Fig. 260, to locate the slits for the prongs as shown at B, Fig. 261.

17. Proceed as in steps 5, 6, 7, and 8.

18. After the purse is lined, assembled, and laced, clamp part 1, Fig. 260, to the edge of the flap by flattening the open end with a mallet as

shown at C, Fig. 261. The lock is shown in place at D, Fig. 261.

Procedure for snap lock

19. Shape the purse. See A, Fig. 263. Locate and punch a hole in the flap of the purse for the post of the snap lock, part 1 in Fig. 262. See A, Fig. 263.

20. Insert the post of the snap lock through the punched hole. Close the lock. Press the closed lock against the body of the purse so that the prongs will locate the slits. See B, Fig. 263.

21. Proceed as in steps 5, 6, 7, and 8.

22. Insert the eyelet, 3 in Fig. 262, into the hole in the flap from the outside. Set the eyelet. (Operation 31.) The purpose of the eyelet is to protect the leather against wear from the post.

23. In closing the purse, place the hole in the flap over the post. See C, Fig. 263. Close the lock.

24. Fig. 264 shows the parts of an alternate snap lock. Attach this lock in the same way as a turn lock. An eyelet is not required as for the lock shown in Fig. 262.

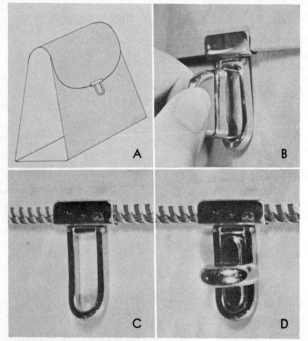

Fig. 261.   Attaching an alternate turn lock

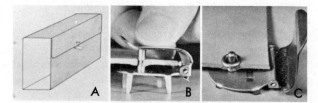

Fig. 263.   Steps in attaching a snap lock

Fig. 262.   Parts of a snap lock

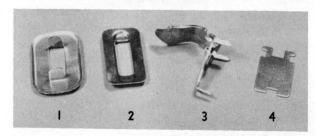

Fig. 264.   Parts of an alternate snap lock

Operation 35   How to cement

Cementing is used for permanent construction and to hold leather in place for either lacing or sewing. Rubber cement is generally used in cementing leather; however, such cements as <u>Barge</u> have a stronger adhesive force. They are permanent cements and are also water- and oil-proof. They may be purchased from a shoe repairman. All cements

are used in much the same way. Follow the specific instructions on the containers.

Procedure for linings

1. Use a jar with a brush top for rubber cement. This will keep it from evaporating. See Fig. 265.

2. To cement a lining to a large surface, pour

cement upon the flesh side of both the lining and cover. Spread it evenly with a piece of cardboard. See Fig. 266. Use a brush for small areas.

3. Apply a coat of cement to both surfaces which are to be cemented together. Let it dry until the shine is gone.

4. In construction which is not to fold, align the two pieces. Press one end of the lining to the cover while you hold the other end of the lining up. Work from the cemented end, pressing and smoothing out the lining. See Fig. 267.

5. Trim the lining even with the cover. Use a knife or scissors.

Fig. 265.   A cement jar

6. In small projects which are to fold, smooth out the lining from one end up to the point where the project is to fold. Fold the cover. Then continue to smooth out the lining from the fold to the other edges. See Fig. 268. This prevents wrinkles at the fold. Trim the lining even with the cover.

7. In large folded projects such as notebooks, apply cement to both the cover and the lining. Center the lining with the binder metal upon the cover. Press the two surfaces together where the cover folds. Place sheets of paper between the cover and lining as shown in Fig. 269-A to keep them from sticking together.

8. Cement one-half of the lining into place, workinf from the center out to the edges. Withdraw the paper as you press the surfaces together.

9. Fold the notebook to shape. Place the unlined half upon the table. Cement this half by pressing the surfaces together as you withdraw the paper. See Fig. 269-B. Trim the lining even with the cover.

10. Start cementing a purse lining to the cover at the bottom fold. Be sure that the lining is centered so that the pockets will be located correctly. After the cementing is completed, trim off the surplus lining even with the cover.

Fig. 266.   Spreading rubber cement

Fig. 268.   Lining a small folded project

Fig. 267.   Smoothing out a lining

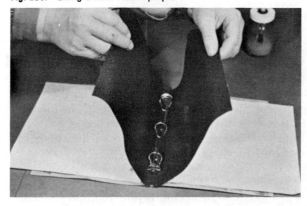

Fig. 269-A.   Using paper to aid in cementing

Fig. 269-B.   Using paper to aid in cementing

Fig. 270.   Applying cement to edges

Fig. 271.   Cementing lining to a folded project

Procedure for edges

11. Apply a strip of cement about ¼″ wide along the edges as shown in Fig. 270 to aid in lacing or sewing.

12. Use a knife to remove or roughen the glazed finish on the grain side of leather if cement is to be applied to it.

13. Cement the edges of linings to one-half of the cover of all folded projects. Then fold the project and press the remaining edges together. This prevents wrinkles at the fold. See Fig. 271.

14. Place all cemented edges upon a smooth surface. Tap them lightly with a smooth hammer or mallet. This makes a stronger union.

Procedure for zippers

15. Apply cement to the flesh side of the leather along the edges of the opening cut for the zipper.

16. Apply cement to the cloth tape of the zipper only where the leather will come in contact with it.

17. Place the zipper upon a table. Starting at the pull end of the zipper, cement the leather to the tape. See Fig. 272. Keep the width of the opening uniform as you press the zipper and leather together.

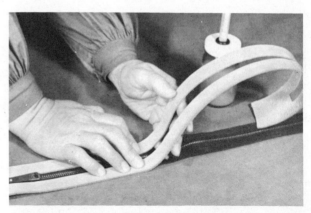

Fig. 272.   Cementing a zipper to leather

Operation 36   How to apply finishes

Read the information about dyes, finishes, and dressings given on pages 17 and 18. All instruction in this operation is general. There are many ways to apply finishes. Follow the special directions on dye containers.

Procedure for dyes

1. Complete all tooling before you apply leather dyes.

2. Clean the leather to remove dirt and the grease caused by fingerprints so that it may be dyed uniformly. Dissolve one teaspoonful of oxalic acid crystals in one pint of water to make a cleaning solution. You may also buy cleaning solutions from supply companies.

3. Apply the cleaning solution with a cellulose sponge.

4. Let the leather dry thoroughly.

5. Pour some dye into a shallow container. Using sheep's wool or cloth, apply the dye in broad strokes. If streaks appear or you have missed small areas, go over the entire surface a second time. Do not try to touch up light spots. See Fig. 273. Always experiment with dye on scrap leather to determine the color desired. Be sure that the scrap leather is like that used in the project.

6. Allow the dyed surface to dry. Remove any excess dye by rubbing with a soft cloth or sheep's

Fig. 273. Applying dye

Fig. 274. Using a small brush to flow on dye

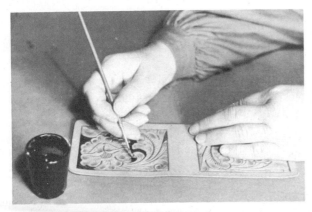

Fig. 275. Dyeing background in a carving

wool. Read the information about clear finishes for a protective coating. See step 23.

7. Use a small camel hair brush to flow dye upon small areas as shown in Fig. 274. You may obtain different tones of colors by flowing one color upon another. Let the dye dry between coats.

8. To dye the background in a carving, apply the dye with a small brush. After dipping the brush into the dye, shake the brush gently to eliminate the possibility of dripping any dye upon the leather. Always bring the brush to the area to be colored from the nearest edge instead of moving it across the project. See Fig. 275. Fiebing's spatter ink is good for delicate backgrounding.

Procedure for edge finishes

There are many ways to finish edges which are not to be laced. Select the procedure which meets your needs.

9. Use a small brush to apply dye to edges of colored leather which will receive little wear. See Fig. 276. Be careful not to get dye on the finished side of the leather.

10. Moisten only the edges of the leather with a sponge. Use a bone folder or the end of a modeler to burnish the edges by rubbing them in a back-

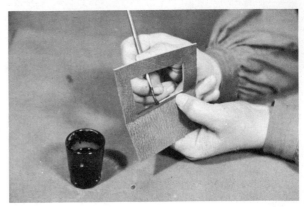

Fig. 276. Dyeing edges

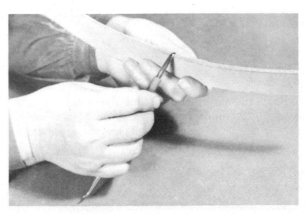

Fig. 277. Burnishing an edge with a modeler

and-forth motion as shown in Fig. 277. This will color the edges and set the fibers.

11. For edges which will receive a lot of wear such as on belts or brief cases, burnish them as in step 10; then apply an edge and casing compound or a gum tragacanth solution to natural leather. Rub the edges with a coarse cloth in one

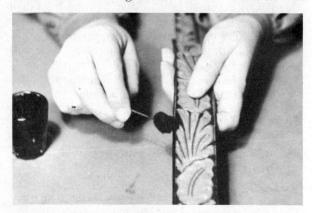

Fig. 278.   Applying edge dye with a dauber

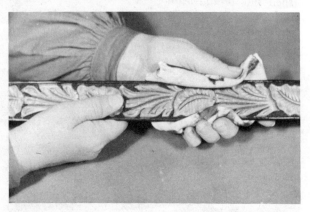

Fig. 279.   Setting edge fibers

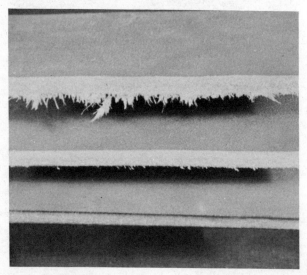

Fig. 280.   Finishing rough edges

direction only, smoothing and setting the fibers. After the fibers are set, rub vigorously in both directions to burnish the edges.

12. Use a dauber to apply Fiebing's edge dye to edges where great penetration of the dye and long wear are desired. See Fig. 278.

13. Apply Fiebing's waterproof edge enamel to edges of wrist watch straps and belts to retard discoloration from perspiration. After the dye is applied, grasp the belt along the edges with a coarse cloth. Pull the belt through to smooth and set the fibers. See Fig. 279.

14. If you use antique finish on a carved surface, apply the finish to the edges also. Set the edge fibers as given in step 13.

15. Sand very rough edges with No. 250 abrasive cloth or fine sandpaper. Complete the sanding by rubbing the edges in one direction only. Be careful not to sand the finished side of the leather. Finish the edges by any one of the preceding methods. Fig. 280 shows a very rough edge, a sanded edge, and a burnished edge.

Procedure for antique finishes

16. If necessary, clean the leather. Allow it to dry.

17. Apply antique finish heavily with a soft brush or a piece of sheep's wool, working the paste well into the carved area. See Fig. 281.

18. Remove the surplus antique finish immediately with a soft cloth, using quick strokes. Leave paste in the stamped areas. You may first remove excess paste with a piece of cardboard as shown in Fig. 282. Save this paste. Experiment on scrap leather to determine the density of color desired.

19. You may secure a two-toned effect on a carved design by removing more of the finish from certain parts of the design than from others with a damp cloth, thus highlighting them by leaving them lighter in color.

Fig. 281.   Applying an antique finish

20. You may also obtain a two-toned effect by first applying lacquer to part of a design or to the entire surface and then applying the antique finish. Remove the surplus as given in step 18.

21. If you use a black antique finish, apply two coats of black dye before you apply the antique finish.

22. Polish all surfaces with a soft cloth after the antique finish has dried. Protect the finish with a clear lacquer. See step 23.

Procedure for protective coatings

23. You should apply a protective coat of clear leather lacquer, liquid or paste wax, or treeing compound to all leather projects whether they have been colored or left natural. Use the recommended thinners for all liquid finishes.

24. Use a soft brush or sheep's wool to apply the finish. Work the finish well into natural leather. Allow it to dry. If you use sheep's wool, pull out or clip off all loose fibers before you apply the finish. See Fig. 283.

25. Apply leather finishes quickly to leather which has been dyed. If you rub the finish into the leather, you may lift the dye.

26. You may add a little dye to either leather lacquer or treeing compound before you apply it to the leather. Mix only a small amount. Always test for color on scrap leather.

Procedure for saddle soap

27. Use saddle soap as a mild cleaner as well as a finish for leather.

28. Apply the soap with a damp sponge. Work up a good lather. Rub the soap well into the leather with a circular motion.

29. Polish the leather with a soft cloth after it has dried.

Fig. 282.   Removing excess antique finish

Fig. 283.   Applying leather lacquer

Procedure for neatsfoot oil

30. Neatsfoot oil is a good preservative for outdoor leather equipment or any leather which will receive heavy use. It is seldom used on carved leather. Apply the oil with sheep's wool.

31. Polish with a soft cloth after the leather has dried. Let the leather dry in direct sunlight if you wish a dark color. The kind of leather will determine the drying time.

Operation 37 How to care for leather articles

The life of all leather articles may be extended if they are given the proper care. Dirt and the lack of sufficient oil in the leather cause deterioration. Proper dressings lubricate the fibers. Do not wait until the leather cracks or shows signs of decay before you start adding the proper oils. Select any of the following procedures for your specific needs.

Procedure

1. For ordinary wear a good leather conditioner such as Lexol should be applied two times a year. Apply it with a soft cloth, let it dry, and polish with a soft cloth. Several light coats are better than a heavy one. This treatment is good for belts, purses, leather chairs, brief cases, and many other leather articles.

2. Use a soft brush to remove loose dirt. Use a damp sponge to work up a lather of saddle soap. Rub this lather well into the leather. If the lather is dirty, remove it from the leather. Then apply clean lather. Allow it to dry on the leather. Polish with a soft cloth.

3. Dry all wet leather slowly. Wet leather is soft. Stitches cut through it easily. As you know, it is readily stretched out of shape.

4. Apply warm neatsfoot oil to work shoes. Rub the oil into the leather with the palm of the hand. Be sure that there is plenty of oil where the soles are fastened to the uppers. Let the shoes dry in a warm place.

5. Wash off all dirt from dress shoes with warm water. Apply a light coat of castor oil with a clean cloth. Rub it well into the leather. Let the shoes dry on shoe trees. Too much oil will prevent the shoes from taking a good polish. You may apply neatsfoot oil to the soles.

6. Once a month apply a light coat of castor oil to patent leather to keep it from cracking.

7. To waterproof leather boots, shoes, and other outdoor articles, apply one of the following formulas:

A. Petroleum jelly	....	2 parts
Paraffin	....	1 part
B. Neatsfoot oil	....	1 part
Paraffin	....	1 part
C. Neatsfoot oil	....	2 parts
Beeswax	....	1 part
D. Neatsfoot oil	....	1 part
Tallow	....	1 part

Heat the ingredients together slowly. Stir thoroughly. Apply the grease with the palm of the hand. Let the shoe soles stand in the grease for ten minutes.

8. Once a year apply purified petroleum jelly to leather bookbindings. Rub the dressing well into the leather. Place the bindings in a warm place 100 degrees F., for about two hours after the oiling. Then polish with a soft cloth.

9. Always give leather an extra supply of oil at points which fold, such as the flaps on brief cases.

10. Repair all broken stitches and lacing at once. If they are not repaired, more strain is placed on other sections of the article.

Hints and tips for the leathercraftsman

Ideas found here may help you enjoy leatherwork more and also be profitable to you.

1. If you skive or stamp through your leather, cement a leather patch over the area on the flesh side. Skive the edges of the patch to a feather edge. See A, Fig. 284.

2. If you punch a hole in the wrong place, cement the punched-out part back into the hole. Place the grain side of the leather upon a smooth surface. Tap the repaired area on the flesh side with a hammer. Place a thin patch over the hole

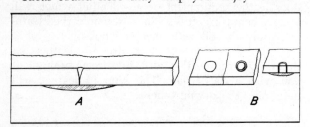

Fig. 284.   Repairing mistakes

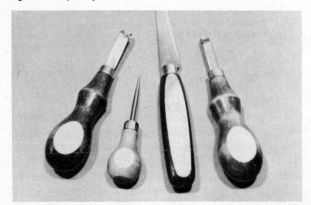

Fig. 285.   Flat spots on handles

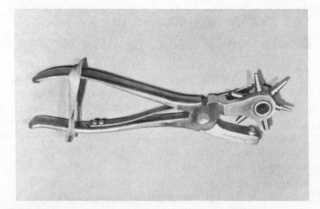

Fig. 286.   Keeping punch handles closed

on the flesh side if the mistake was made in light-weight leather. See B, Fig. 284.

3. If you are short of leather but have a piece that has a very thin spot, cement a patch over this area on the flesh side. Be sure to feather the edges of the patch. You can then tool or carve over the area.

4. After casing leather for carving, apply a *very* light coat of Lexol before you cut with the swivel knife. The leather will cut more easily but its color will be somewhat darker when you apply the finishes. Try this out first on scrap leather.

5. Flatten a spot on the handles of knives and other tools so that they will not roll off the bench. See Fig. 285.

6. Make a leather band to keep revolving punch handles together when the punch is not in use. See Fig. 286.

7. Stick harness and glover's needles into corks for safekeeping. See Fig. 287.

8. Place small pieces of colored cellophane tape around stamps and handles of tools for easy identification.

9. Remove thread from the needle and use a sewing machine to make stitch holes for hand sewing.

10. If the leather is hard and you have difficulty in punching the holes for hand sewing, moisten the leather slightly. If the leather is too wet, the stitches will pull through.

11. Use a hand drill to twist flax thread if you have a large amount to make. Prepare the thread as instructed in Operation 28. Tie several knots in one end of the strands. Place these knots in the drill chuck. See that the strands are equal in length. Fasten the other ends in a vise. Turn the drill, twisting the strands into thread as shown in Fig. 288. Taper the end and rewax the thread. Short strands were used in order to photograph this operation.

12. If grommets are not available, try setting two eyelets. Use the eyelet setter to spread one eyelet as shown at A in Fig. 289. Do not strike the setter too hard. Punch a hole in the leather. Insert this eyelet. Place the second eyelet so that it starts to go on the inside of the first one. Drive it slowly into place as shown at B, Fig. 289. Turn the leather over and set the second eyelet so that it will fit snugly against the first eyelet as shown at C, Fig. 289.

13. Wrap cotton around the end of a toothpick. Use it to apply dye to small areas or edges.

14. Use a toothpick to apply cement to very small areas such as splices in lace.

15. If the hammer leaves marks on the leather as you form square bends, place a piece of scrap

Fig. 287.   Needles placed in corks

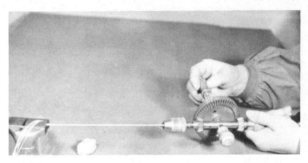

Fig. 288.   Twisting flax strands

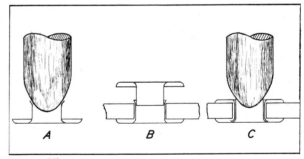

Fig. 289.   Using eyelets for grommets

leather over the leather to be formed. Strike the scrap piece with the hammer.

16. Try a power sander with a fine abrasive belt to sand and smooth edges in finishing.

17. Apply neutral edge and casing compound to the fuzzy flesh side of a belt to smooth it out.

18. Use spring clips or spring clothespins to aid in holding leather in place as you assemble a project.

19. Make friends with your shoe repairman. He will be able to help you with your sewing and cementing problems.

PROJECTS

For best results,
first look at the photograph of the project
and the layout drawing.
Next read *all* of the steps
in making the project
in order to get a general idea
of how it is constructed.
Then start with step A in the procedure
and follow the directions.
References are made to the operations
which give the needed "How-to-Do" instruction.
In some of the projects,
a reference to a certain operation is given
only the first time the information is needed.
Always read all of each step
in the procedure before working,
not just a part of it.

Project 1 Car key cases

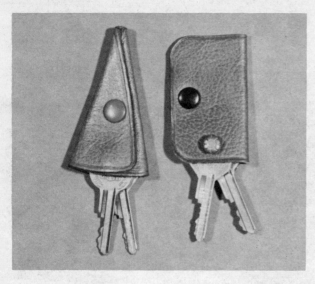

Fig. 290. Car key cases

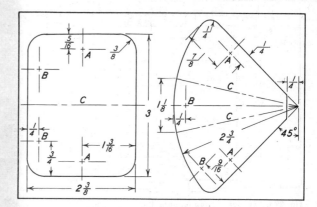

Fig. 291. Layout of car key cases

Use 2- or 3-oz. scrap leather to make these key cases. They will hold two keys.

Procedure

A. Lay out on heavy paper one of the key cases as shown in Fig. 291. Cut out the paper pattern.

B. Place the pattern upon the leather. Trace around it. (Operation 3.)

C. Cut out the stock. (Operation 5.)

D. Use the edge creaser on all edges. (Operation 17.)

E. Crease a line at C, Fig. 291, on the flesh side to aid in folding the key case. (See Fig. 117.)

F. Locate and set a 16-line snap fastener as shown at A, Fig. 291. (Operation 33.)

G. Locate and punch holes for a ½″ binder post as shown at B, Fig. 291. (Operation 30.)

H. Fold the key case. Fasten the binder post in position.

I. Set the edges. Apply a finish. (Operation 36.)

Project 2 Luggage tags

Use 3- to 4-oz. scrap leather to make this project. Select either style shown in Fig. 292.

General procedure

A. Lay out on heavy paper either Fig. 293 or 294. Cut out the paper pattern.

B. Place the pattern upon the leather and trace around it. (Operation 3.)

Fig. 292. Luggage tags

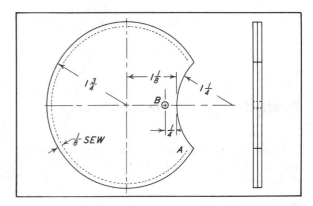

Fig. 293. Layout of round luggage tag

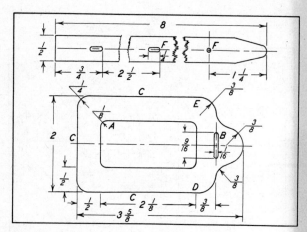

Fig. 294. Layout of strap luggage tag

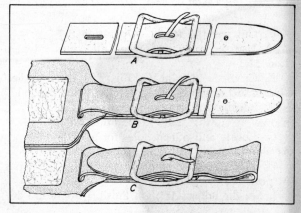

Fig. 295. Fastening strap to buckle

C. Cut out the stock. (Operation 5.) Since two pieces are required for each tag, cut the second piece a little larger. You will trim it to size later.

Procedure for round tag

D. You may tool or stamp initials on this tag. (Operation 9.)

E. Cement the edges. (Operation 35.) Do *not* cement the edges of the curved opening.

F. Trim the second piece even with the first piece.

G. Sew the tag, starting ¼″ from the opening as shown at A, Fig. 293. (Operation 28.)

H. Punch a No. 5 hole for a bead chain at B, Fig. 293. (Operation 30.)

I. Finish the edges and surfaces. (Operation 36.)

J. Insert an identification card. Put the bead chain through the hole and fasten the tag to your luggage.

Procedure for strap luggage tag

K. Cut out the window opening in the first piece which was cut in step C. Use a No. 8 punch for the rounded corners as shown at A, Fig. 294. Cut between the punched holes. (Operations 5 and 30.)

L. Use a No. 0 punch to round the ends of the slot shown at B, Fig. 294. Cut between the holes.

M. Cement the edges of the three straight sides of the window piece to the second piece. (Operation 35.)

N. Trim the edges of the back piece even with the front piece. Cut the slot at B in the back piece. Fig. 294.

O. Color the luggage tag if you wish. (Operation 36.)

P. Cut thong slits for ³⁄₃₂″ lace ⅛″ from the edges marked C in Fig. 294. (Operation 23.)

Q. Starting at D, Fig. 294, lace with the whip-stitch around to E. (Operation 24.)

R. Lay out and cut the strap.

S. Punch the hole and cut the two slots in the strap as shown at F, Fig. 294. Use a No. 0 punch. (Operation 30.)

T. Finish the edges and surfaces. (Operation 36.)

U. Insert an identification card. For protection place a thin piece of celluloid over the card.

V. Place the strap with the flesh side up in a ½″ strap buckle as shown at A, Fig. 295. Insert the end of the strap through the slot in the tag and fasten the strap to the buckle as shown at B, Fig. 295. To hold the tag to your luggage, place the tapered end of the strap through the buckle as shown at C, Fig. 295.

Project 3   Bookmarks

Make this project for your first attempt at tooling or carving. Use 3- to 4-oz. natural tooling calf or cowhide.

Procedure

A. Lay out the size of the bookmark on the leather. Fig. 297. (Operation 3.)

B. Cut out the stock. (Operation 5.)

C. Prepare the leather for tooling or carving. (Operation 6.)

D. Copy a design from the back of this book. (Step 19, Operation 1.)

E. Transfer the design. (Operation 8.)

Fig. 296. Bookmarks

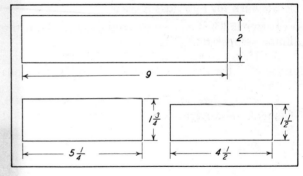

Fig. 297. Layout of bookmarks

F. Do outline tooling or carving. (Operation 9 or 15.)

G. Finish the bookmark. (Operation 36.)

Project 4 — Eyeglasses cases

Use 2- to 3-oz. leather to make the cases. The one in Fig. 299 makes a good case for sunglasses. It was made from tooling steerhide. The case in Fig. 300 was made from ostrich-grained calf.

General procedure

A. Lay out on heavy paper the two parts for Fig. 299 or the pattern for Fig. 300. Cut out the pattern.

B. Place the pattern upon the leather. Trace around it with an awl. (Operation 3.)

C. Cut out the stock. (Operation 5.)

Procedure for sunglasses case

D. Crease a line along the top edge of the front piece. Tool this piece if you wish. (Operations 9 and 17.)

E. Cut a skiver lining larger than the back piece. Cement it to the flesh side of the back piece. (Operation 35.)

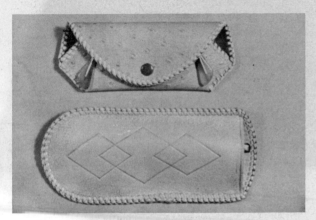

Fig. 298. Eyeglasses cases

F. Trim the lining even with the cover.

G. Cement the edges together.

H. Thong the edges for ³⁄₃₂″ lace. Lace with the single buttonhole stitch. (Operations 23 and 25.)

I. Finish the case and the open edge. (Operation 36.)

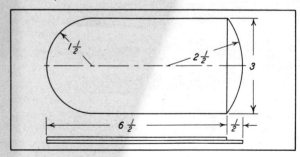

Fig. 299. Layout of sunglasses case

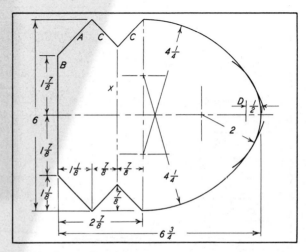

Fig. 300. Layout of eyeglasses case

Procedure for eyeglasses case

J. Cement a skiver lining to the cover. Trim the lining. (Operation 35.)

K. Thong edges A and B, Fig. 300, for ³⁄₃₂″ lace. Lace with the single buttonhole stitch. (Operations 23 and 25.)

L. Skive edges C. Fold the case at X, Fig. 300. Cement these edges together. (Operations 18 and 35.)

M. Thong these edges and the flap. Lace as in Step K.

N. Set the cap and eyelet of a 16-line snap fastener at D, Fig. 300. (Operation 33.)

O. Put the glasses into the case. Bring the flap over. Press the cap firmly to mark the location for the spring and post.

P. Set the spring and post.

Q. Finish the case. (Operation 36.)

Project 5   Wrist watch straps

In Fig. 301 the strap on the watch was made from cordovan. Above the watch are straps made from alligator, lizard, and cobra. These straps cost only a few cents to make. Make the plain strap first. You may change the dimensions of the straps as desired.

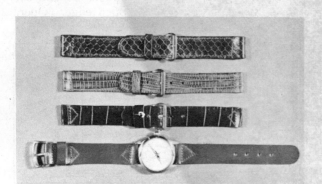

Fig. 301. Wrist watch straps

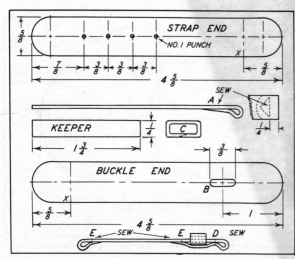

Fig. 302. Layout of wrist watch straps

Procedure for Cordovan strap

A. Lay out and cut three pieces from cordovan or 3-oz. calf as given in Fig. 302. (Operations 3 and 5.)

B. Skive one end of the strap end. Fold at X, Fig. 302. (Operation 18.)

C. Cement this end into place. Sew as shown at A, Fig. 302. (Operations 35, 28, and 29.)

D. Skive the ends of the buckle strap. Punch No. 1 holes at the ends of the slot shown at B, Fig. 302. Cut out the slot between holes. (Operations 30 and 5.)

E. Make a keeper as shown at C, Fig. 302. Form the keeper to fit over the thickness of two straps. Cement the joint together.

F. Cement and sew the buckle end into place as shown at D, Fig. 302.

G. Place the keeper into position. Cement and sew the two places at E, Fig. 302.

H. Finish the edges of the straps. (Operation 36.)

I. Punch the holes in the strap end.

J. Remove the old band from the watch by pushing the sliding pins in the removable bars.

K. Assemble the watch strap by placing the tongue of the buckle into the slot opening. Slide the spring bar through the loop end of the strap and the loop in the buckle tongue. Place the buckle over one end of the spring bar. Depress the other end of the spring bar and let it snap into place.

L. Insert the spring bars into the other ends of the watch strap and fasten it to the frame of the watch.

Procedure for other strap assemblies

Alligator

M. Construct this strap as given above.

Lizard

N. Cut out the strap end 9¼″ long. Cement a reinforcement strip at D, Fig. 303.

O. Cement the strap together. Sew around it as shown at A, Fig. 303. (Operation 29.)

P. Reinforce the buckle end strap at E as shown at B, Fig. 303. Sew as in step O.

Q. Cut out the slot for the buckle tongue. See step D. Fold the end back at X, Fig. 303.

R. Sew at F. Insert the keeper over the strap. Make the keeper as given in step E.

S. Sew at G. Finish the edges of the strap. (Operation 36.)

T. Punch the holes in the strap end. Attach to the watch as given in steps J, K, and L.

Cobra

U. Cut two straps from 2-oz. calf; the length should be as given in Fig. 302.

V. Cobra is very thin. Cut two cobra straps wider and longer than the calf straps as shown at C, Fig. 303. Notch the rounded ends as shown at H.

W. Cement the cobra to the calfskin. (Operation 35.)

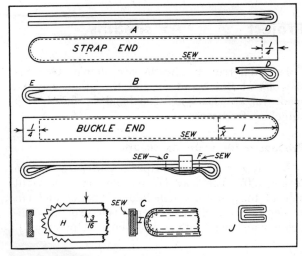

Fig. 303. Alternate layouts of watch straps

X. Cement a strip of cobra over the back of the strap. Cement this strip as shown at I.

Y. Sew as in step O. Make a keeper from cobra by cementing a strip together as shown at J.

Z. Complete the strap as in steps Q, R, S, and T.

Project 6 Checkbook cover

Make the checkbook cover from 3- to 4-oz. leather. The one shown in Fig. 304 was made from 4-oz. tooling steerhide. As in all projects, the procedure of construction may be changed. Work out an original decorative design if you so desire. Change the dimensions as needed to fit your checkbook.

Procedure

A. Lay out on the leather the three pieces needed for the checkbook cover. See Fig. 305. (Operation 3.)

B. Cut out the stock. (Operation 5.)

C. Cement the edges of the two crosspieces to the flesh side of the cover. (Operation 35.)

D. Thong for ³⁄₃₂″ lace. (Operation 23.)

E. Lace with the double buttonhole stitch. (Operation 26.)

F. Locate and set the cap and eyelet of a 16-line snap fastener at A, Fig. 305.

G. Locate and set the spring and post at B, Fig. 305.

H. Apply neutral antique finish to the cover. (Operation 36.)

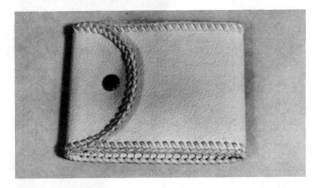

Fig. 304. Checkbook cover

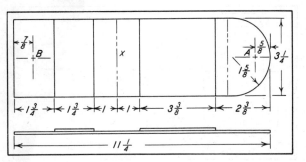

Fig. 305. Layout of checkbook cover

Project 7   Ax sheaths

Two different ax sheaths are shown. One fits the official Boy Scout ax and the other may be made for any hand ax. The hand ax sheath is a "quickie" to make.

Procedure for scout ax sheath

A. Lay out on heavy paper a pattern as shown in Fig. 307. You may lay out and cut the right side of the pattern. Then fold the paper and cut to get the rest of the pattern. You may also develop your own pattern as given in Operation 1.

Fig. 306.   Ax sheaths

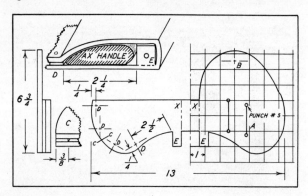

Fig. 307.   Layout of scout ax sheath

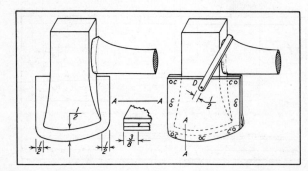

Fig. 308.   Layout of hand ax sheath

B. Trace the pattern on 5- or 6-oz. cowhide. (Operation 3.)

C. Cut out the stock. (Operation 5.)

D. Punch No. 5 holes for the slits to fasten the ax sheath to a belt as shown at A, Fig. 307. (Operation 30.) Cut between the holes.

E. Moisten and fold the leather as shown at X, Fig. 307. (Operation 20.)

F. Cut a stitch-block ⅜" wide as shown at C. Cement it into place between the edges of the sheath from D around the curved part to D. (Operation 35.) A stitch-block is used so that if the leather should pull apart at the sewing a sharp edge would not cut the thread.

G. Set four rapid rivets at D, Fig. 307. (Operation 32.)

H. Fold the two small flaps E over and set one rapid rivet.

I. Sew between the rapid rivets at D. (Operation 28.)

J. Set the cap and eyelet of an 18-line snap fastener on the flap at B. (Operation 33.)

K. Place the ax into the sheath. Fold the flap over the ax to mark the location for the spring and post. Set the spring and post.

L. Apply neatsfoot oil to the sheath. (Operation 36.)

Procedure for hand ax sheath

M. Lay the ax upon heavy paper and trace the size of the pattern. See Fig. 308.

N. Lay out the pattern on 6-oz. leather. Cut out two pieces. (Operations 3 and 5.)

O. Cement a ⅜" stitch-block between the curved edges of the sheath as shown at A-A, Fig. 308.

P. Set seven rapid rivets as shown at C, Fig. 308. (Operation 32.)

Q. Fasten one end of a ½" strap to the back of the sheath with a rapid rivet.

R. Bring the strap over the ax handle and set a snap fastener as shown at D, Fig. 308. (Operation 33.)

S. Apply neatsfoot oil to the sheath. (Operation 36.)

T. You can make a similar sheath for a double blade ax.

Project 8   Knife sheath

You may make a sheath for any knife if you follow the instructions. The sheath in Fig. 309 is for the official Boy Scout knife.

Procedure

A. Lay out on heavy paper the pattern B for the knife sheath. (Operation 1.) Use the allowances as shown in Fig. 310.

B. Trace around the pattern on 6- or 7-oz. cowhide. (Operation 3.)

C. Cut out the stock. (Operation 5.)

D. Cut out part C slightly larger than needed.

E. Cement a 5⁄16″ stitch-block from D to E on part B as shown at A-A, Fig. 310. (Operation 35.)

F. Cement part C to the stitch-block and the long straight side of part B.

G. Trim part C even with part B.

H. Set three rapid rivets at D, E, and F. (Operation 32.)

I. Sew between the rivets. (Operation 28.)

J. Punch No. 5 holes and cut the slits between the holes as shown at G, Fig. 310. (Operations 5 and 30.)

K. Make a ½″ strap from 4-oz. leather.

L. Put the knife into the sheath. Place the strap around the handle to determine the length of the strap and the location of the rivet.

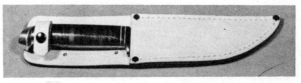

Fig. 309.   Knife sheath

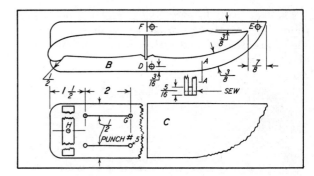

Fig. 310.   Layout of knife sheath

M. Rivet the strap to part B as shown at H, Fig. 310.

N. Set a 16-line snap fastener on the strap. (Operation 33.)

O. Cut off the surplus length of the strap.

P. Finish all edges. (Operation 36.)

Q. Apply neatsfoot oil to the sheath.

Project 9   Book cover

Make the book cover from 3- to 4-oz. tooling calf. The front of the one shown in Fig. 311 was decorated with an over-all stamped design.

Procedure

A. Fold a piece of paper around a book so that 7⁄16″ will extend at the top and bottom of the book. Turn the paper pattern under the cover one-half the width of the cover.

B. Lay out the size of the pattern on the leather. (Operation 3.)

C. Cut out the stock. (Operation 5.)

D. Work out a stamped design on the front of the cover. (Operation 14.)

E. Apply a finish to the cover. (Operation 36.)

F. Turn the leather back at both ends of the cover, thus forming a pocket at each end for the

Fig. 311.   Book cover

cover of the book.

G. Cement the edges of the pockets. (Operation 35.)

H. Lace the top and bottom edges of the book

cover with Florentine lacing. (Operation 27.)

I. You may reinforce the edges of the cover between the pockets by pulling a piece of lace under the stitches on the inside of the cover.

Project 10   Key case

The key case in Fig. 312 is for a 6-hook key frame. Key cases of various sizes may be made. There are several decorative designs in the back of this book.

Fig. 312.   Key case

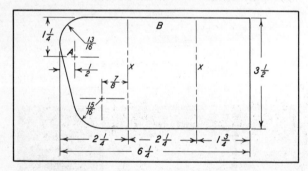

Fig. 313.   Layout of key case

Procedure

A. Lay out a paper pattern as given in Fig. 313.

B. Make a permanent template if several key cases are to be made. (Operation 2.)

C. Cut out 4-oz. tooling calf. (Operation 5.)

D. Copy a design for the key case from the back of the book. (See Fig. 69.)

E. Carve the design. (Operation 15.)

F. Apply antique finish. (Operation 36.)

G. Cut out a lining from lightweight calf.

H. Center the swivel part of the 6-hook key frame so that it is ¼″ from the edge of the lining. It should be centered between the two lines marked X in Fig. 313 as shown at B.

I. Set three eyelets to hold the key frame to the lining. (Operation 31.)

J. Cement the lining to the cover. As you cement, fold the cover at X. (Operation 35.)

K. Trim the lining even with the cover.

L. Use ³⁄₃₂″ lace to lace the key case with the double buttonhole stitch. (Operation 26.)

M. Apply a clear leather lacquer. (Operation 36.)

N. Set the cap and eyelet of a 16-line snap fastener at A, Fig. 313. (Operation 33.)

O. Place one finger on the inside of the case to make allowance for the keys. Close the case. Press firmly on the cap to mark the leather for the position of the spring and post.

P. Set the spring and post.

Project 11   Coin purse

You may change the shape and size of the coin purse and the decorative design. The purse in Fig. 314 is only a suggestion of what you can do.

Procedure

A. Lay out on tracing paper the size of the coin purse as given in Fig. 315.

B. Copy on the tracing paper a pattern for the carved design. You may select one from the back of the book. (See Fig. 69.)

C. Cut out the leather. (Operation 5.)

D. Carve the design. (Operation 15.)

E. Cement a very thin lining to the cover. Fold the cover at X as you cement. (Operation 35.)

Fig. 314. Coin purse

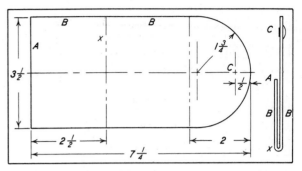

Fig. 315. Layout of coin purse

F. Trim the lining even with the cover.

G. Using ³⁄₃₂″ lace, lace the open edge with the whipstitch as shown at A, Fig. 315. (Operation 24.)

H. Skive edges B, Fig. 315. (Operation 18.)

I. Fold at X. Cement B to B.

J. Lace the edges with the double buttonhole stitch. Do not lace the bottom folded edge. (Oper-

ation 26.)

K. Set the cap and eyelet of a 16-line snap fastener at C, Fig. 315. (Operation 33.)

L. Close the flap. Locate the position for the spring and post. Set the spring and post. (See steps 6 and 11, Operation 33.)

M. Apply clear lacquer if this was not done in Step D. (Operation 36.)

Project 12   Ladies' billfold

The billfold shown in Fig. 316 was made from ostrich-grained calf.

Procedure

A. Lay out the six pattern pieces as shown in Fig. 317.

B. Cut out the leather. (Operation 5.)

C. Cement a lightweight lining to the cover. (Operation 35.)

D. Skive all edges which are to be cemented together to reduce the thickness of the leather. (Operation 18.)

E. Fold the flaps on the lining at X, Fig. 317.

Cement on the flesh sides as shown at A, Fig. 318. (Operation 35.)

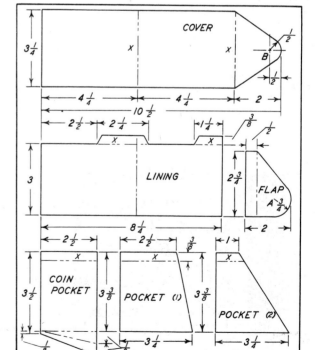

Fig. 317. Layout of ladies' billfold

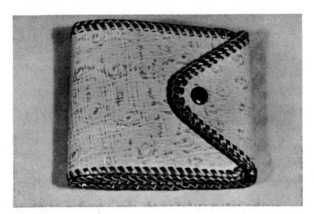

Fig. 316. Ladies' billfold

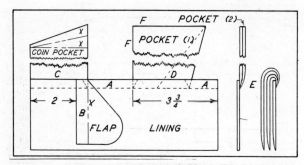

Fig. 318. Assembly of pockets and lining

Fig. 319. Inside of billfold

F. Cement the grain side of the edge of the coin pocket flap to the lining as shown at B, Fig. 318. If a cement such as Barge is used, you will not need to sew any of the cemented edges. If you use rubber cement, sew all cemented parts if they are not to be laced. (Operation 29.)

G. Cement the flesh side of the edge of the coin pocket as shown at C, Fig. 318.

H. Cement the flesh side of the edge of pocket 1 as shown at D, Fig. 318.

I. Cement the flesh side of the edge of pocket 2 over pocket 1.

J. Fold the leather at X on the coin pocket. Bring it over the flap at B. Cement it to the edges of the lining.

K. Bring pocket 1 over and cement edges F to the lining 3¾" from the end.

L. Bring pocket 2 over and cement it to pocket 1 as shown at E, Fig. 318.

M. Fold the flap at X. Set a 12-line cap and eyelet on the flap as shown at A, Fig. 317. (Operation 33.)

N. Bring the flap over. Locate the position of the spring and post on the coin pocket. Set the spring and post. (See steps 6 and 11, Operation 33.)

O. Cement the lining with the pockets to the cover. Fig. 319 shows the inside of the billfold.

P. Lace the billfold with the double buttonhole stitch. Use ³⁄₃₂" lace. (Operation 26.)

Q. Set the cap and eyelet of a 16-line snap fastener on the cover at B, Fig. 317.

R. Fold the billfold to locate the position of the spring and post. Set the spring and post.

S. Apply a clear finish. (Operation 36.)

Project 13 Billfold

This billfold was made from tooling calf with a carved design. The background was colored.

Fig. 320. Billfold

Procedure

A. Lay out and cut the cover from tooling calf. See Fig. 321. (Operations 3 and 5.)

B. Carve the design. (Operation 15.)

C. Cement a thin lining to the cover. (Operation 35.)

D. Lay out and cut pockets 1 and 2. Cut a right and a left of each pocket.

E. Skive all edges which are to be cemented. (Operation 18.)

F. Crease a line on the open edges of all pockets. (Operation 17.)

G. Fold pockets 1 on the fold line. Cement the edges marked A together. See Fig. 321.

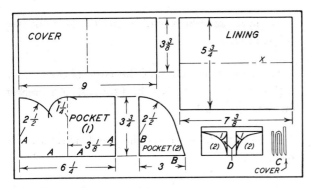

Fig. 321. Layout of billfold

H. Cement two edges of pocket 1 to the cover. See C, Fig. 321.

I. Cement edges B of pockets 2 to pockets 1. See D, Fig. 321.

J. Using 3/32" lace, lace with the double button-hole stitch. (Operation 26.)

K. Cut out a lightweight pocket lining. Fold at X, Fig. 321.

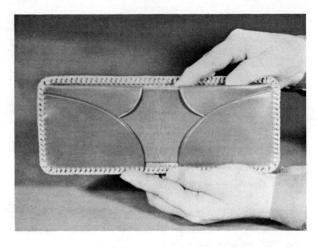

Fig. 322. Inside of billfold

L. Cement the flesh sides of the lining together.
M. Trim the lining even. Insert it into pockets 1 as shown at D, Fig. 321.
N. Since this type of lining is loose, it will adjust to billfolds of any length. See Fig. 322.

Project 14   Pocket secretary

This project was made from tooling calf. The pockets were made from calf of a different color.

Procedure

A. Lay out and cut the cover from tooling calf. Fig. 324.

B. Copy a design for this project from the back of this book. (See Fig. 69.)

C. Carve the design. (Operation 15.)

D. Cut out the four pockets.

E. Crease a line on all open pocket edges. (Operation 17.)

F. Cement a thin lining to the cover. (Operation 35.)

Fig. 323. Pocket secretary

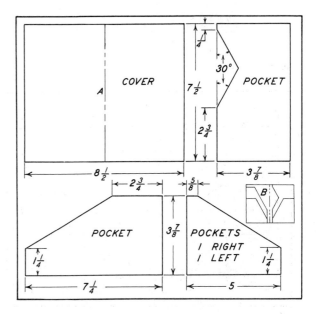

Fig. 324. Layout of pocket secretary

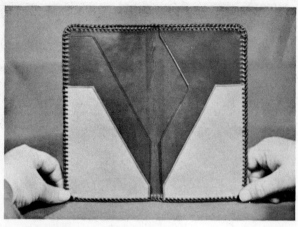

Fig. 325.   Inside of pocket secretary

G. Skive all edges which are to be cemented. (Operation 18.)

H. Cement the edges of the large pockets to the edges of the cover. See B, Fig. 324. All pockets open to the inside.

I. Cement the edges of the small pockets to the large ones.

J. Using the double buttonhole stitch, lace the pocket secretary with ³⁄₃₂″ lace. (Operation 26.)

K. See the pocket secretary opened in Fig. 325.

Project **15**   Gusset coin purse

Use steerhide of 2- to 3-oz. weight to make this project. Tool the cover if you wish.

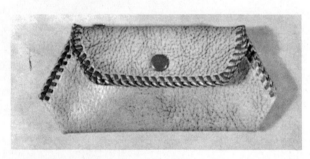

Fig. 326.   Gusset coin purse

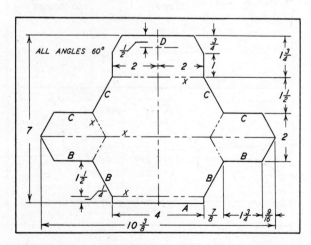

Fig. 327.   Layout of gusset coin purse

Procedure

A. Lay out the pattern on heavy paper as shown in Fig. 327.

B. Place the pattern upon the leather. Trace around it. (Operation 3.)

C. Cut out the stock. (Operation 5.)

D. If you are not tooling the cover, apply a finish. (Operation 36.)

E. Cement a thin lining to the flesh side. (Operation 35.) Cut the lining so that it will fit along line X at edge A, Fig. 327.

F. Trim the lining even with the cover.

G. Fold edge A back over the lining. See Fig. 327. (Operation 19.) You may crease or sew this edge. (Operation 17 or 29.)

H. Skive edges B. Cement them together. (Operations 18 and 35.)

I. Lace edges B with the single buttonhole stitch. Use ³⁄₃₂″ lace. (Operation 25.)

J. Skive edges C. Cement them together.

K. Lace edges C and the flap.

L. Set the cap and eyelet of a 16-line snap fastener at D, Fig. 327. (Operation 33.)

M. Close the flap. Locate the position of the spring and post. (Step 6, Operation 33.) Set the spring and post.

Project 16 Belts

Three styles of belts are shown in Fig. 328. Select the style you like and follow the instructions for it. You may vary the width of the belts as you wish.

General procedure

A. Determine the length of the belt as shown in Figs. 329, 330, and 331.

B. Use a ready-cut 8-oz. strap leather belt blank or cut out the belt yourself. (See Fig. 103, Operation 5.) The billet ends in Fig. 331 and all leather keepers should be made from 6-oz. strap.

C. Shape all billet ends. Bevel all edges. (Operation 16.)

D. Use an edge creaser on all edges. (Operation 17.)

E. Stamp or carve the belt. (Operation 14 or 15.)

F. Burnish all edges. Apply a finish. (Operation 36.)

Procedure for regular belt

G. Cut the slot for the buckle tongue and punch No. 4 holes at D, Fig. 329. (Operation 30.)

H. Set eyelets and studs of 16- or 18-line Segma belt snaps at A. Set the buttons and sockets at B. Fig. 329. Belt snaps are made for heavy leather. (Operation 33.)

I. Make a keeper as shown at C, Fig. 329. Fasten it with a belt staple or sew it. (Operation 20.) Fasten the buckle into place as shown at E, Fig. 329.

Procedure for western type belt

J. Cut a slot at C, Fig. 330. Punch No. 4 holes in billet end A, Fig. 330. (Operation 30.)

K. Set eyelets and studs of Segma snaps at D. Set the buttons and sockets at E, Fig. 330. See step H.

L. Fasten the metal tip to the end of billet A.

M. Fasten one or two metal keepers and the buckle into place.

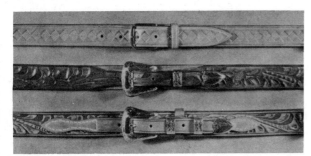

Fig. 328. Belts

Procedure for ranger type belt

N. Sew billet ends A and B as shown in Fig. 331.

O. Cut the slot for the buckle at D in billet B. Cut a slot in the end of the belt at C for this

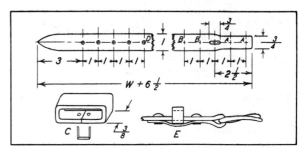

Fig. 329. Layout of regular belt

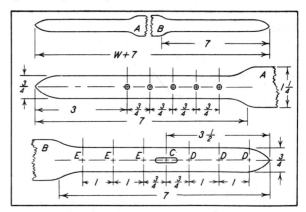

Fig. 330. Layout of western belt

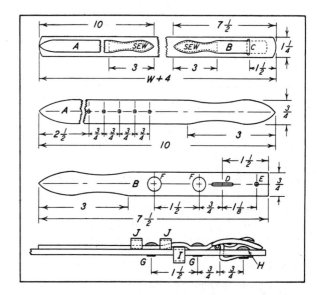

Fig. 331. Layout of ranger belt

billet end as shown in Fig. 331. Punch No. 4 holes in billet A. (Operation 30.)

P. Set the eyelet and stud of a Segma snap on the grain side of billet B as shown at E, Fig. 331. Set buttons and sockets at F and in the belt end at H. Set eyelets and studs at G. (Operation 33.)

Q. Make the keeper as shown at I in Fig. 331 or as instructed in step I.

R. Fasten the metal tip to the end of billet A.

S. Fasten two metal keepers, the leather keeper I, and the buckle into place on the billet as shown in Fig. 331.

Project 17   Zipper billfold

Make this billfold from tooling calf. Decorate the cover by any of the various methods.

Procedure

A. Lay out and cut the cover as shown in Fig. 332. (Operations 3 and 5.)

B. Tool or carve a design on the cover. (Operations 9, 10, 11, or 15.)

C. Lay out and cut the four pockets and the lining.

D. Cut the opening in the lining for the zipper.

E. Crease a line on the edges of the pockets at A. (Operation 17.)

F. Skive all edges which are to be cemented. (Operation 18.)

G. Cement the zipper to the lining. Sew along the ends and upper edge. (Operations 35 and 29.)

H. Cement the pockets to the lining. Sew them to the lining along the lower edge of the zipper.

I. Fold the cover at X. Cement the edges of the lining to the cover.

J. Apply finishes. (Operation 36.)

K. Lace with ⁹⁄₃₂″ lace, using the double buttonhole stitch. (Operation 26.)

L. Fig. 333 shows the inside of the billfold.

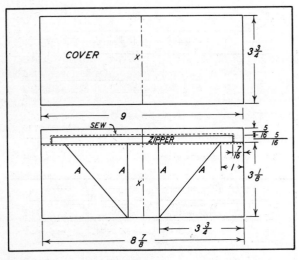

Fig. 332.   Layout of zipper billfold

Fig. 333.   Inside of zipper billfold

Project 18   Picture frame

The picture frame in Fig. 334 was made from ostrich-grained calf. It folds compactly and may be carried easily when you travel.

Procedure

A. Lay out and cut two pieces of leather as given in Fig. 335. Cut the back piece oversize. It will be trimmed to size later. (Operations 3 and 5.)

B. Lay out and cut the openings.

C. Cut line A, Fig. 335, from the sewing line at B near the top of the frame to the sewing line at B near the bottom of the frame. The pictures will be inserted into the frame through these openings.

Fig. 334. Picture frame

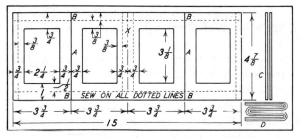

Fig. 335. Layout of picture frame

D. Cement the edges of the front to the back as shown at C. Trim the back even with the front.

E. Sew on all dotted lines as shown in Fig. 335. (Operation 29.) Tie the ends of the thread at the edges. The lacing will cover the knots.

F. Lace with ³⁄₃₂″ lace, using the double button-

hole stitch. (Operation 26.) Be careful not to cut the sewing when you thong for the lacing.

G. Fold the frame at X and A so that it will have the shape shown at D, Fig. 335. (Operation 20.)

H. Insert the pictures.

I. Read Operation 37 on how to care for leather articles.

Project 19 — Drawstring purse

The lower part of the purse shown in Fig. 336 was made from 8-oz. strap leather and decorated with outline tooling. It might be carved or left plain. The top part is hair calf, but suede would work equally well.

Procedure

A. Lay out and cut 8-oz. strap leather. See A, Fig. 337. (Operation 5.)

B. Develop a decorative design. (Operation 1.)

C. Tool or carve the design. (Operations 9 or 15.)

D. Apply a finish. (Operation 36.)

E. Cut the base from pine. Sand the edges smooth. See B, Fig. 337.

F. Form the tooled leather around this base to get the exact length. Cut off the surplus leather.

G. Punch No. 0 round holes in the ends of the bottom piece as shown at D, Fig. 337. (Operation 30.)

H. Apply cement to the ends. Butt them together. This will hold the ends together while you lace them.

I. Using ⅛″ lace, lace the ends together with a cross-stitch. Start at the bottom hole as shown at E, Fig. 337, and lace to the top.

Fig. 336. Drawstring purse

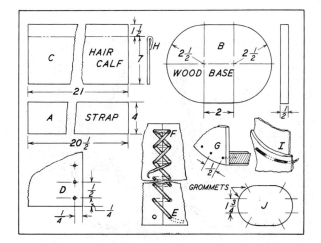

Fig. 337. Layout of drawstring purse

J. Lace across the two top holes twice. Then fill in the cross-stitch from top to bottom. See F, Fig. 337.

K. Cement thin leather to the top and bottom of the wooden base. Trim the leather even with the edge of the base.

L. Place the bottom part of the purse over the base. Use No. 16-½" escutcheon pins to nail the leather to the base. Use a No. 53 drill to drill holes for the pins. This will keep the wood from splitting. See G.

M. Lay out and cut the hair calf as shown at C. Fold the top edge as shown at H.

N. Punch No. 0 holes ⅜" apart and ¾₆" from the bottom edge of the hair calf. (Operation 30.)

O. Punch No. 0 holes in the top edge of the strap leather, spacing them as in step N.

P. Place the hair calf on the inside of the bottom part. Lace the two together with a running stitch. See I. Start to lace at the cross-stitching on the bottom part.

Q. Lace around to the starting point. Let the ends of the hair calf overlap ½". Cut off the surplus.

R. Punch holes as in step N in the ends of the hair calf. Lace from the bottom to the top.

S. Set eight No. 1 grommets 1" from the top edge and 1¾" apart. Place four grommets on each of the curved ends as shown at J, Fig. 337. (Operation 31.)

T. Cut two drawstrings from 6-oz. leather. Make them ⅛" wide and 30" long.

U. Dye the strings if you so desire. Finish the edges as in step 11, Operation 36.

V. String the purse by running a drawstring through the four grommets at one end, then along the straight side and through the grommets at the opposite end. Run the second string through in the opposite direction from the first one.

W. Determine the correct length of the drawstrings. Cut off any surplus. Knot the ends of the strings. Pull the strings in opposite directions, thus closing the purse.

Project 20 Scuffies

Many styles of scuffies may be made. Fig. 338 shows a very plain pair. Heels and heel straps may be attached. The straps may be stamped or carved. Use originality in this project.

Procedure

A. Place the right foot upon a piece of heavy paper. Trace around it with a pencil. Smooth out the lines in the outline of your foot. Cut out this pattern.

B. Trace around the pattern on 8-oz. leather two times. Turn the pattern over and trace around it two more times. Cut out the four pieces. (Operations 3 and 5.)

C. Determine the length of the toe straps by using a strip of heavy paper 1½" wide. Place one end of the paper strip under the right foot. Bring the paper over the instep and down under the foot on the other side. Allow 1" at each end of the paper where it touches the floor.

D. Cut four straps from 6-oz. strap leather 1½" wide and the determined length.

E. Crease a line on the edges. (Operation 17.) Finish the edges of the straps. (Operation 36.)

F. Place the right foot upon the right sole. Determine the best position of the straps by trying them. Mark the position on the sole. Cut slots along the edges of the sole for the straps. See A, Fig. 339.

G. Skive one end of two straps. Put the skived ends through the slots and fold the skived ends as shown at B. (Operations 18 and 20.)

H. Put the other ends of the straps through the slots on the other side. Place the foot upon the sole and determine the exact length of each strap. Bend the surplus end of the strap under the sole.

Fig. 338. Scuffies

Be sure to check the length of the straps when you are standing. Cut off any surplus. Skive as shown at B.

I. Use these two straps to lay out the length of the straps for the left foot. Since you have both right and left straps, place the straps with the grain sides together in order to cut at the desired angle on the ends of the left straps.

J. Place the grain sides of the top right and left soles together to locate the position of the slots in the left sole. Cut the slots.

K. Cement the straps to the top soles. Then cement the bottom soles to the top soles with the flesh sides together as shown at C. (Operation 35.)

L. Trim the edges even.

M. Sew around the edges. (Operation 28.)

N. If a cushioned sole is desired, cement a piece of ½″ thick sponge rubber between the soles. The sponge rubber should come to within ½″ of the

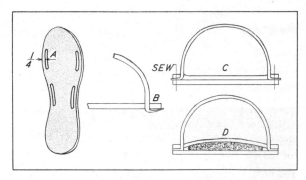

Fig. 339. Assembly of scuffies

edge of the sole. It will flatten when the soles are put together. See D.

O. Finish the edges of the soles with sole and heel dressing or neutral casing compound. (Operation 36.)

P. Apply a finish to the scuffies.

Project 21 Album

A filler 10″ x 13″ fits the album in Fig. 340. You may make albums of other sizes. The procedure will be the same, but you must make allowances for the cover.

Procedure

A. Lay out and cut the front and back of the cover from 8-oz. strap leather. (Operations 3 and 5.) See Fig. 341.

B. Carve one piece for the front cover. The design is in the back of the book. (Operation 15.)

C. Apply finishes to the front and back. (Operation 36.)

D. Gouge out the leather on the flesh side of the cover at the wide end border as shown at A, Fig. 341. The cover will fold at this point. (Operation 20.)

E. Cement lining to the front and back. Trim the lining even with the covers. (Operation 35.)

F. Set two No. 0 grommets in the front and back covers as shown at B. See C, Fig. 341.

G. Lace the edges with ⅜″ Florentine lace. (Operation 27.)

H. Cut a tie from 6-oz. strap leather. Finish the edges. (Operations 5 and 36.)

I. Insert telescope eyelets, D, into the grommets and through the holes in the filler paper. Tie the album with the thong made in step H.

Fig. 340. Album

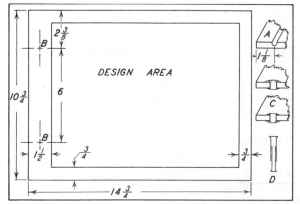

Fig. 341. Layout of album

Project 22   Small notebook

Make the notebook from 4- to 6-oz. leather. The one illustrated was made from 4-oz. tooling calf.

Fig. 342.   Small notebook

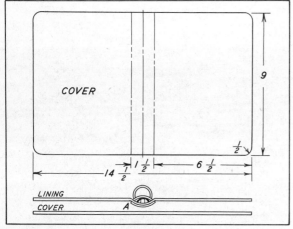

Fig. 343.   Layout of small notebook

Procedure

A. Cut out the leather for the cover. See Fig. 343. (Operation 5.)

B. Copy a design from the back of the book. (Operation 1.)

C. Carve the cover. (Operation 15.)

D. Apply antique finish. (Operation 36.)

E. Cut a lining slightly larger than the cover.

F. Center the metal part A, Fig. 344, on the lining to locate the holes to be cut for projections 1, 2, 3, and 4.

G. Cut out the openings.

H. Place part A under the lining with projections 1, 2, 3, and 4 through the holes.

I. Place the rings, B in Fig. 344, over the lining and part A. Insert the keys, C, to hold the two parts together.

J. Center the lining with the binder metal upon the cover. See A, Fig. 343. Cement the lining and cover together. (Operation 35.)

K. Trim the lining even with the cover.

L. Lace with ³⁄₃₂″ lace, using the double button-hole stitch. (Operation 26.)

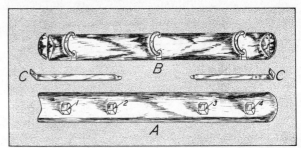

Fig. 344.   Loose-leaf binder metal

Project 23   Hand-sewed purse

Use 6-oz. strap for this purse. The one shown in Fig. 345 was left plain and treated with only saddle soap.

Procedure

A. Cut out the cover as shown in Fig. 346. (Operation 5.)

B. Fold the cover at right angles on all lines marked X. (Operation 20.)

C. Reinforce the top and bottom of the purse as shown at A. Use belly leather. Skive the edges thin. Cement into place. (Operations 18 and 35.)

D. Cut two pieces for the handle.

E. Curve the handle straps slightly and cement the flesh sides together.

F. Sew along the edges of the handle and to within 1″ of each end of the handle. Keep the stitches ⅛″ from the edges. (Operation 28.)

G. Trim and finish the edges of the handle. (Operation 36.)

H. Locate the position of the handle on top of the purse. Cement it into position as shown at C.

I. Sew the handle to the top. This will complete the sewing along the edges at the ends of the handle.

J. Cut out the lock tab. Line it with thin chrome calf to within 1″ of the top. Skive all edges of the lining very thin. Turn back ¼″ along all but the top lining edge. Notch out the corners as shown at B, Fig. 346. Cement the folded edges. Then cement the lining to the tab.

K. Sew the lining to the tab. Do not cut off the thread.

L. Cement the unlined edge of the tab to the purse flap as shown at D. Sew the tab to the flap. Do *not* sew across the tab along the edge of the flap.

M. Cut out two gussets as given in Fig. 346. To check the gusset size for your purse, measure the width between the two sides at the bottom and the height at the front of the purse. Make allowances for the folded edges as shown at E. Notch the corners at the bottom of the gussets as shown at E. Make right angle folds along the sides and bottoms of the gussets. (Operation 20.)

N. Cement a lining to the gussets but not to the folded edges. Finish the top edges like B.

O. Sew the top edges of the gussets.

P. Cut a chrome calf lining for the purse large enough to make folded edges along all open edges.

Q. Make folded edges on the lining for the flap. Cement this part of the lining to the purse. Next, cement the lining to the back, the bottom, and halfway up the front of the purse.

R. You can now determine the location of the folded edge on the lining at the top edge of the front part of the purse. Make the folded edges and cement the lining into place.

S. Sew across the edge of the front part of the purse. Also sew around the flap from the point where the top back corner of one gusset will be

Fig. 345. Hand-sewed purse

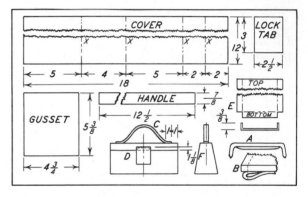

Fig. 346. Layout of hand-sewed purse

located to the corresponding point on the other side of the flap. Sew across the lock tab.

T. Trim and skive the lining where the gussets will be cemented.

U. Cement only ¼″ of the folded edges of the gussets into place. Trim off the surplus. The surplus was needed to aid in making the folded edges. If you have difficulty with the gussets and flap, moisten the gussets slightly at F at the top center. They will then shape themselves in their natural way.

V. Sew in the gussets.

W. Locate and set the lock. (Operation 34.)

X. Saddle soap the purse. (Operation 36.)

Project 24 Carved purse

Use 6-oz. strap leather to make this purse and lightweight calf for the lining.

Procedure

A. Make a paper pattern for the flap end-and-back part. Use 1″ squares to lay out this pattern.

The front part of the purse is the same as 5¾″ of the back section. See Fig. 348. Cut out the leather. (Operations 3 and 5.)

B. Copy the carving design for the purse from the back of the book. (Operation 1.)

C. Carve the purse. (Operation 15.)

Fig. 347. Carved purse

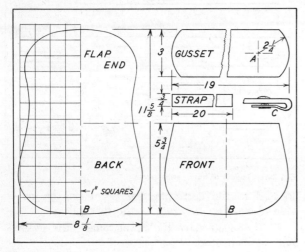

Fig. 348. Layout of carved purse

D. Apply a finish to the carving. (Operation 36.)

E. Cut out the gusset and strap. See Fig. 348. Crease a line along the edges of the strap. (Operation 17.) Finish the strap edges. Apply a finish to the gusset and strap.

F. Fasten a strap hanger to each end of the gusset at A, Fig. 348.

G. Cut out lining for the two carved parts and the gusset.

H. You may want to sew a pocket, 3″ x 5″, to the back lining 2″ up from the bottom edge. (Operation 29.)

I. Cement the linings to all parts. (Operation 35.)

J. Punch round holes around all three parts, ³⁄₁₆″ from the edges. Space the holes ¼″ apart. (Instruction starts at step 10, Operation 30.)

K. Lace the ends of the gusset and the top edge of the front part with ⅛″ lacing, using the whipstitch. (Operation 24.)

L. Find the center hole on each edge of the gusset. Using a short piece of lace, tie the gusset at these holes to the front and back parts at B, Fig. 348.

M. Tie the gusset into place at every eighth hole.

N. Lace the purse with the double buttonhole stitch. (Operation 26.)

O. Attach the lock. (Operation 34.)

P. Skive each end of the strap. Fold 1″ of each end as shown at C. (Operation 20.)

Q. Set a 16-line snap button at each end of the strap. Fasten the strap to the hangers. (Operation 33.)

Project 25 Wastebasket

Make the wastebasket from 10-oz. strap leather. Notice the simplicity of the decorative design.

Procedure

A. Cut out strap leather 11″ x 25⅛″. The basket is 8″ in diameter. (Operation 5.)

B. Use a No. 5 edge creaser to crease lines at A, Fig. 350. Place a straightedge upon the leather as a guide. Use both projections on the end of the creaser. You will make one deep, wide mark and one fine line. Use plenty of force to make these lines. (Operation 17.)

C. Lace the ends of the wastebasket together by following steps G, H, I, and J in Project 19.

D. Cut a piece of wood 8″ in diameter for the bottom. Use wood ¾″ thick.

E. Sand the wood. Fit to the inside of the wastebasket.

F. Cement a piece of calf to the top of the wooden base. (Operation 35.)

G. Use ½″-shank antique hammered upholstery nails to fasten the leather to the wooden base. Drill holes slightly smaller than the nails to aid in driving the nails into the wood. See B, Fig. 350.

H. Cement a piece of suede to the bottom. Trim it even with the sides. Be careful not to cut the strap leather.

I. Finish the top edge. (Operation 36.)

Fig. 349. Wastebasket

J. Mix together equal parts of neatsfoot and castor oils. Apply a thin coat to the wastebasket. Let the sun darken the leather.

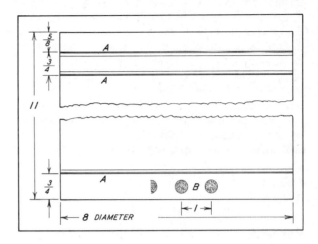

Fig. 350. Layout of wastebasket

Project 26   Cigar box

Make the cigar box from 8-oz. strap leather. Design a box to any dimensions you may desire, but follow the given procedure. Notice the combined decorative effect of the creased lines, the saddle stitching, and the escutcheon pins.

Procedure

A. Cut a piece of strap leather 6″ x 11″. (Operation 5.)

B. Crease some lines on this piece for decoration. See step B in Project 25.

C. After you have creased the desired lines, cut off a 1″ x 11″ strip for the lid.

D. Lay out and drill No. 55 holes in the ends of both pieces as shown at E and F, Fig. 352.

E. Form the pieces into cylinders.

F. Cut the ends at a slight angle as shown at D so they will fit together snugly at the seam.

G. Cement the ends together. (Operation 35.)

H. Use 6-cord flax thread to sew or lace the seam. Fasten the thread in a harness needle. Start

Fig. 351. Cigar box

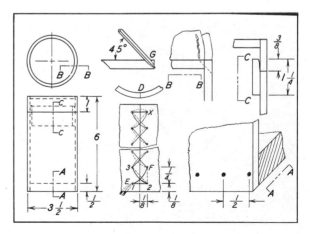

Fig. 352. Layout of cigar box

sewing at E, and go up through hole 1, down through hole 2, up through hole 3, etc. Sew to the top; then go straight across to hole X. Go down through this hole. Crisscross back down to F. From F, go straight down to hole 2. Go up through hole 2, down through hole 3, etc., to the top. Go across to hole X and up through it. Crisscross back down to E, completing the stitch. The stitch will be the same on the inside of the box as the outside.

I. Cut a wooden bottom for the box. Sand it smooth and fit it inside the bottom of the cylinder.

J. Fasten the leather to the bottom with No. 16-½″ brass escutcheon pins. Use a No. 53 drill to drill holes for the pins. See A-A in Fig. 352.

K. Cut out a round piece of leather for the lid.

L. Use an awl to make holes around the piece for sewing as shown at G. Be sure that the awl is held at 45 degrees.

M. Cement this round part to the lid. Sew as shown at B-B. The holes which you punched in the top part will aid in keeping the awl at the correct angle when you punch the holes through the side part of the lid. (Operation 28.)

N. Cut a piece of leather to fit inside the box as shown at C-C. Round and finish the top edge. This piece helps to center and hold the lid in place.

O. Cement this piece to the inside of the box.

P. Apply neatsfoot oil to the box. (Operation 36.)

Project 27   Electric clock

This project was designed for a 3⅜″ electric clock unit. Ostrich-grained calf was used to cover a wooden core.

Procedure

A. Shape a piece of pine as given at A, Fig. 354. Cut the round opening and put the slight angle on the base. Sand all edges smooth.

B. Test the size of the hole with the clock unit.

C. Cut a strip of leather wider than the core and long enough to go around the two ends and two sides. (Operation 5.)

D. Start cementing this leather to the core at the center as shown at B, Fig. 354.

E. Notch the corners. Bring the ½″ surplus

leather down over the edges, cementing it to the face and back as shown at C.

F. Cement this strip around the core to the starting point. Cut off the surplus leather and make a butt joint.

G. Cut leather to cover the front and back of the core. Cut it ½″ oversize. Do not cut the opening for the clock unit.

H. Make a ¼″ folded edge along two edges. (Operation 19.) Place the leather on the front or back to check for size. See D. Fold the other edges. Notch and roll the corners as shown at E.

I. Cement the front piece to the core.

J. Drive No. 16-½″ brass escutcheon pins around

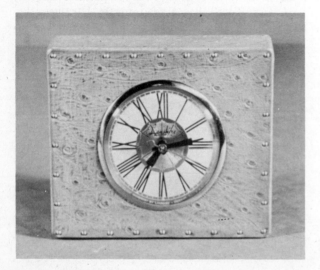

Fig. 353.　Electric clock

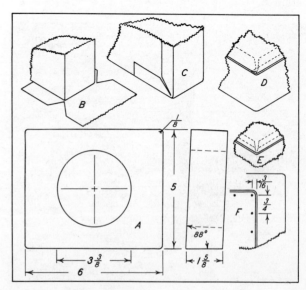

Fig. 354.　Layout of electric clock

the edges to decorate the case as shown at F. Drill holes with a No. 53 drill to keep the wood from splitting. If necessary, slightly increase or decrease the space between the pins as you near the end.

K. Cut the opening.

L. Cover the back as you did the front.

M. Insert the clock unit. Make the necessary electrical connections. Fasten the back plate into place.

N. Read Operation 37 on how to care for leather articles.

Project 28   Lamp

The lamp base has a wooden core which is covered with ostrich-grained calf. The shade size is 11″ x 11″ x 16″. Follow the dimensions given for this lamp or develop your own design.

Procedure

A. Cut a piece of pine to the size given in Fig. 356. Slightly round all corners except the bottom edges.

B. Bore all holes as shown at A, B, C, and D.

C. Make a 20-gauge sheet iron plate. See Fig. 356. Drill a hole through it. Recess it into the wood

over hole A. See A-A in Fig. 356. Be sure that the plate is flush with the wood. Fasten it into place with two small flat-head wood screws. This plate will hold a rotary canopy switch.

D. Cut a piece of leather slightly larger than the height and distance around the lamp. (Operation 5.)

E. Cement this leather to the lamp core with a joint at one corner. (Operation 35.)

F. Cut the leather even with the top and bottom of the wooden core.

G. Cement a piece of leather to the top. Cut it even with the sides and ends.

H. Make two trim pieces long enough to go around the lamp and four pieces the height of the lamp. See E for size and detail. Skive and make folded edges. (Operations 18 and 19.)

I. Starting at the center of the top back edge, cement the trim around the top edges of the lamp as shown at F. Notch the top half of the trim at the corners.

J. Cement the trim around the bottom of the lamp.

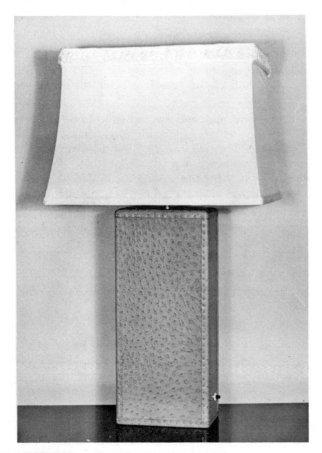

Fig. 355. Lamp

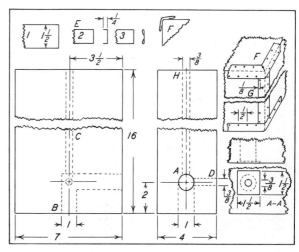

Fig. 356. Layout of lamp

K. Cut and fit the trim at the four corners between the top and bottom trim as shown at G. Cement into place.

L. Drive No. 16-½″ brass escutcheon pins along the edges of all trim. Keep them about ⅛″ from the edge. You may want to vary this distance slightly. Drill No. 53 holes to aid in driving the pins. Do *not* drive pins into the bottom of the lamp.

M. Cut away the leather which covers the holes at D and H and the hole in the metal plate.

N. Use an adjustable lamp cluster. Have the shade at a height which barely allows the top of the lamp base to show.

O. Wire the lamp. Screw a ⅛″ socket bushing into the hole at D.

P. Cement a piece of leather over the bottom of the lamp. Cut the edges even with the trim on the bottom.

Project 29 Gadget bag

The size of the gadget bag in Fig. 357 is 6″ x 9″ x 12″.

Fig. 357. Gadget bag

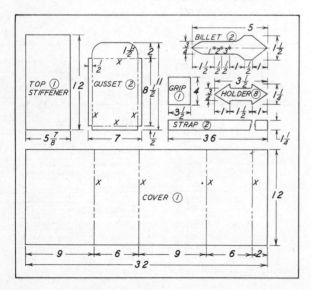

Fig. 358. Layout of gadget bag

Procedure

A. If you wish to design your own gadget bag, see Operation 1.

B. If you make the bag in Fig. 357, cut out all parts as shown in Fig. 358. Cut the handle grip from calf, the billets and strap holders from 6-oz. strap leather, and all other parts from 8-oz. strap. The number with a circle around it indicates the number of pieces needed.

C. Fold the cover at right angles on all lines marked X, Fig. 358. (Operation 20.)

D. Fold the gussets at X on the grain side. The rounded ends of the gussets will fold to the inside of the bag.

E. Cement and sew the top stiffener to the top of the bag between the folds as shown at A, Fig. 359. (Operations 35 and 28.) Use five stitches per inch and a 6-cord flax thread. Either make the thread or buy it from a shoe repairman.

F. Cement ¼″ of the folded edges of the gussets to the cover as shown at B in Fig. 359. Trim the surplus edges of the gussets even with the edges of the cover. The surplus was needed to aid in making the folded edges.

G. Set rapid rivets to reinforce the top corners of the gussets and the cover as shown at C, Fig. 359. (Operation 32.)

H. Sew the gussets to the cover.

I. Fold a 7″ section at the center of the 36″ handle straps. Cement this section. Set rapid rivets as shown at D, Fig. 359. Crease a line along the edges of the straps. (Operation 17.) Burnish the edges. (Operation 36.)

J. Crease a line around the edges of the grip. Burnish the edges. Cement the grip to the center of one of the folded handles at E, Fig. 359.

K. Sew between the rivets on both handles.

L. Crease the open edges of the eight strap holders. Burnish all edges. Cement the strap holders into place. Sew as shown at F, Fig. 359.

M. Crease and burnish the edges of the billets.

N. Lay out and punch the holes in one billet. (Operation 30.) Cement and sew the billet at G.

O. Cut off 1½″ of the strap end of the second billet. Skive and turn back 1″. Cut a slot for the tongue of a ¾″ strap buckle. Set a rapid rivet at H to hold the buckle in place.

P. Cement and sew the buckle end at I.

Q. Place the straps through the holders. The handle with the grip goes to the back of the bag. Adjust the straps so that the handle part comes together at the center of the bag top and 3″ above it.

R. Bring the grip around the handles. Locate and set two 16-line snaps as shown at J. (Operation 33.)

S. Make a 24-gauge metal frame for the ends and bottom of the bag. Form as shown at K. Check to see that the frame fits inside the bag.

T. Cover the frame with thin leather. Cut the leather 2″ larger than the frame. Apply cement to both the frame and the leather. Notch the leather at the corners. Stretch the leather as you turn back 1″ of leather to the back of the frame. If you moisten the leather slightly, it will stretch more easily and be very tight on the metal when it dries.

U. Cement the covered metal frame to the bottom and the gussets of the bag.

V. Drill two holes through the gussets and the metal frame. Set two rapid rivets at the top of the gussets as shown at L.

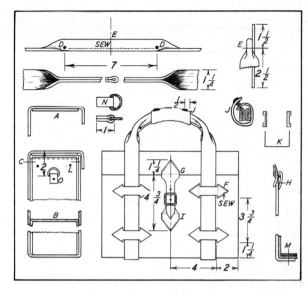

Fig. 359. Assembly of gadget bag

W. Fasten the ends of the handle straps to the bottom of the bag. Drill two holes through the end of each strap, the bottom of the bag, and the metal frame. Set the rivets as shown at M.

X. If a shoulder strap is desired, use ¾″ dee rings and make hangers as shown at N. Use rapid rivets to fasten the hangers to the bag as shown at O.

Y. Make a ¾″ shoulder strap the desired length. Fasten a ¾″ spring snap to each end of the strap with a rapid rivet. Snap the shoulder strap to the dee rings. You may make a shoulder pad from sponge rubber and leather if you wish.

Z. Apply neatsfoot oil to the gadget bag. (Operation 36.)

Project 30 — Carved brief case

Although this is a large project, it is easily constructed if the instructional material is closely followed. However, it is assumed that the individual has done considerable leatherwork before he attempts this brief case.

Procedure

A. Lay out and cut 2-oz. steerhide to cover the metal frame. Cut the gussets from 4-oz. steerhide and all other parts from 8-oz. strap leather. The circle with a number in it shows the number of pieces needed.

B. Carve the front and back. (Operation 15.) The design is in the back of the book.

C. Fold the front and back and sew to the bottom

Fig. 360. Carved brief case

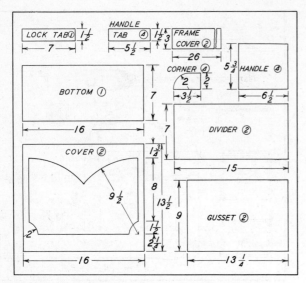

Fig. 361.   Layout of brief case

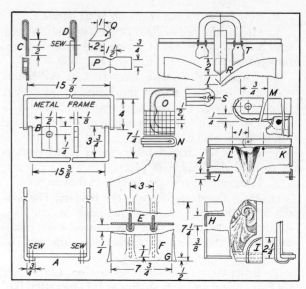

Fig. 362.   Assembly of brief case

as shown at A in Fig. 362. (Operations 20 and 28.)

D. Make the metal frame. Drill a ³⁄₁₆″ hole in the ends at B, Fig. 362.

E. Moisten the 2-oz. steerhide. Stretch and cement it to the metal frame as shown at C, Fig. 362. (Operation 35.) Cut the leather from the holes in the metal.

F. Sew the top edge of the front and back to the leather around the metal frame as shown at D. (Operation 28.) The cover will extend beyond the ends of the frame after it is sewed. Tie the frame together at the holes.

G. Sew the dividers to the gussets as shown at E to within 1″ of the bottom edge as shown at F, Fig. 362. Moisten the leather at the folds.

H. Trim the edges of the gussets from the top corners to the bottom. They should be the dimension shown at G. The top of the gussets should be 9″ wide. The sewing stretched the gussets out of shape. Fold the side and bottom edges of the gussets as shown at H.

I. Burnish the edges of the corner bumpers. Cement and sew them to the cover as shown at I. The outer edges will be sewed with the gussets.

J. Cement thin leather to a piece of sheet metal. Cement the metal to the bottom of the case for a stiffener. The metal is 6¾″ x 15¼″.

K. Cement ¼″ of the folded edges of the gussets to the sides and bottom as shown at J. If the gussets are too long, shorten them. Cement them to the ends of the metal frame as shown at K. You *must* have surplus leather at the center of the gusset. Set rapid rivets at L. (Operation 32.) Trim the edges of the gussets even with the side and bottom edges of the cover. Sew the edges of the gussets to the case.

L. Untie the ends of the frame. Trim and sew the leather at the ends as shown at M.

M. Fold and cement the leather for the handles as shown at N. Lay out a pattern and trace the handles on the leather. Sew inside the line as shown at O. Cut the handles and finish the edges. (Operation 36.) You can cut the handles on a band saw if you wish.

N. Fold, cement, and shape the handle tabs as shown at P. Finish the edges, Set a rapid rivet ½″ from the end at Q.

O. Shape one end of the lock tab. Finish the edges. Cement and sew it to the side of the cover which was sewed to the longer part of the metal frame. See R, Fig. 362.

P. Insert ¾″ rectangular loops into the ends of the handle at S, Fig. 362, and into the ends of the handle tabs. Use an awl to open up the leather for the loops.

Q. Locate and cement the handle tabs to the same side of the case as the lock tab. The top of the tabs is even with the top edge of the side of the cover as shown at T. Sew the tabs to the case.

R. Locate the second handle and tabs so that the handles will center and be even when the case is carried. Cement and sew the tabs to the case.

S. Fasten a three-position narrow case lock on the front in the same position as the lock tab was sewed on the back. (Operation 34.)

T. Cut the lock tab to the correct length. Fasten the metal tip to the end of the tab.

U. Finish the brief case. (Operation 36.)

V. Fasten the ends of the frame together with ⅝″ No. 9 copper belt rivets. Place one or more burrs on the rivets between the frame ends to space them apart.

Project **31**   Table lighter

The construction of this project is very different. It is a good project to use up scrap pieces of heavy leather. An Evans table lighter unit was used.

Procedure

A. Using wood glue or Barge cement, fasten together enough 2¾″ x 2¾″ scraps of 8- to 10-oz strap leather to make a piece 2⅝″ high. See A, Fig. 364. Be sure that the grain side is up on all pieces.

B. Turn the laminated piece on a wood or metal lathe. Since the leather tends to spring, the tools must be sharp and fine cuts made.

C. Drill or bore on the lathe the hole for the lighter cup. The diameter B, Fig. 364, is a tight fit.

D. Sand the lighter with fine sandpaper.

E. Apply edge compound or antique finish and burnish the lighter. (Operation 36.)

F. Cement a piece of suede to the bottom. Trim it even. You may set the edges of the suede with edge compound.

Fig. 363.   Table lighter

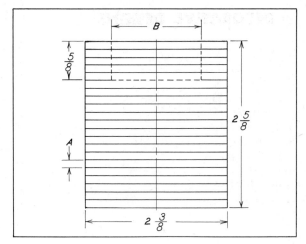

Fig. 364.   Layout of table lighter

DECORATIVE DESIGNS

These designs are included
for the convenience of those
who have neither the time nor the desire
to make their own designs.
As you develop skill in leathercraft,
you will want to make your own decorative designs.
First try using parts of these designs,
making various combinations of them
or changing their proportions.
Soon you will be decorating your projects
with your own ideas.
Study the photographs on the following page.
Observe the number of variations
in the carved flowers and leaves.
The carving designs by Ken Griffin
were stamped with the beginner in mind.
Tracing patterns are found on one page
with the carving of the same design
on the opposite page.
By following the carved design,
the beginner will soon learn
the use of the various stamps.

Above: Tooling   Below: Doodle Panel of Carving

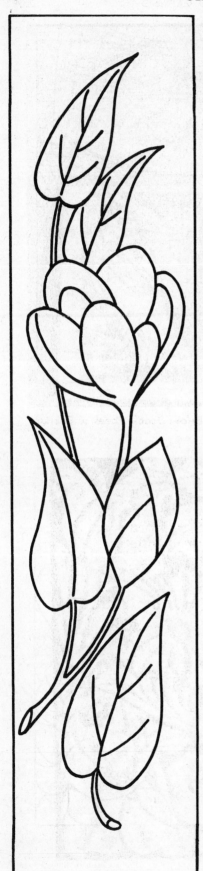

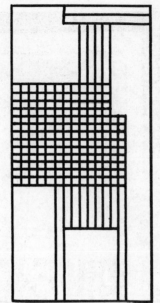

Left: **Bookmark**   Above and below: **Key Case Panels**

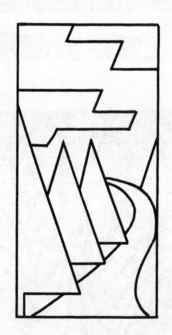

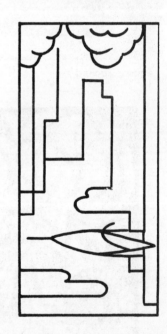

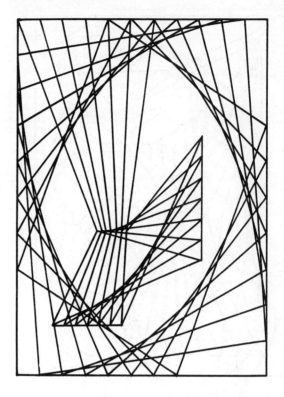

Billfold Panels

Billfold Panels

Belts

Belts

Billfold

Billfold

Left: Bookmark   Above: 4-Hook key case   Below: Bookmark

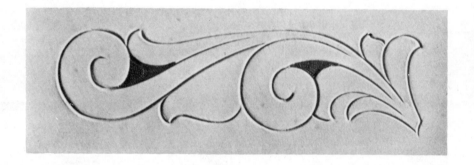

Below: 6-Hook key case

Left: Bookmark   Above: 4-Hook key case   Below: Bookmark

Below: 6-Hook key case

Coin Purse

Billfold

Coin Purse

Billfold

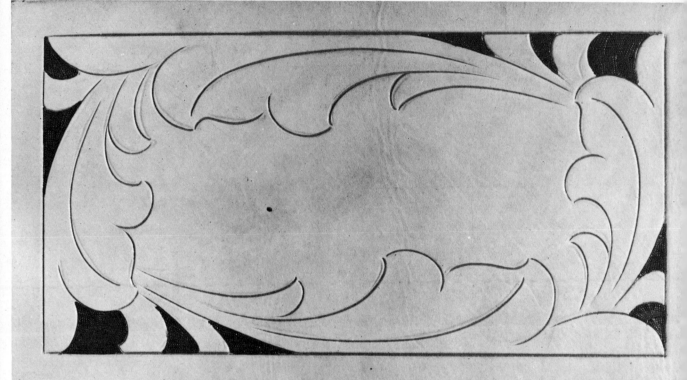

Pocket Secretary

Pocket Secretary

Notebook

Notebook

Notebook

Notebook

Album

Album

Front of Purse

Purse

Purse   Flap End

Front of Purse

Purse

Flap End

Brief case

Brief case

Belt Billets

Belts

Billfold   Billfold

History of leather

In ancient times

No one actually knows when primitive man first made leather or just what method he used. Earliest authentic historical records go back nearly 5000 years. From carved stone tablets left by the Egyptians of that time, we learn that they knew about leather and valued it equally with gold and ivory. They even considered it worthy of tribute to their kings and gods. Perfectly preserved leather articles have been found in Egyptian tombs known to be over 3000 years old.

There are numerous references to leather in the Bible. The legends and tales of the ancient Greeks and Romans contain frequent references to leather. At one time among the ancient Romans, leather was used as the basis of their money. From the Latin word "pecus" meaning "hide", we get our English word "pecuniary" meaning "pertaining to money."

The early American leather worker

It was not necessary for the white man to bring the art of leather tanning to America, for the first explorers found that the Indians were quite skillful in this art. It is not known just how or when they gained their knowledge and skill. The work was done chiefly by the squaws.

Different tribes used different methods to prepare the leather. They generally piled the skins until decay started. Sometimes wood ashes were mixed with the skins. The decay loosened the hair which was then scraped off by hand as was the flesh from the under side. Then oil and animal brains were pounded into the skins. Following this, the skins were often smoked. The American Indian was especially skillful in making buckskin. This type of leather has never been equalled for its softness or ability to turn water.

Leather workers were among the earliest American colonists and extensive use was made of leather. Many articles of clothing, door hinges, fire buckets, tableware, and coach springs were just a few things commonly made of leather in colonial times.

Thousands of years before, the ancient Hebrews had been the first people to develop the method of tanning leather by using oak bark. No decided changes in this method of tanning were made until the latter part of the eighteenth century. Then people learned that oak bark was not the only source of tanning materials. They found that bark from hemlock and chestnut trees, as well as various other plant substances, were all satisfactory for tanning leather. This was important to the American leather worker since hemlock trees were plentiful.

Changes in manufacturing methods

Near the end of the nineteenth century, an American chemist discovered that chromium salts acting upon hides produced leather different from that produced by the bark tanning method. Other experiments proved that it was necessary for this new type of leather to be treated with soaps and oils. Thus our modern method of chrome tanning was developed. It soon became the chief way of producing leather.

About the same time Americans invented machines which greatly changed the methods of working with leather. These machines made it possible for one man to do many times the work he could formerly do by hand. Perhaps the most important machine was one which would split leather to any desired thickness, thus making available at least twice the amount of usable leather. Other machines took care of the de-hairing, fleshing, and cleaning.

Manufacture of leather

Pelts of animals arriving at a tannery may be classified according to their size: (1) *hides* which comes from large animals such as cows or horses, (2) *kips* which come from undersized animals of the same group, and (3) *skins* which come from small animals such as sheep, goats, and calves.

Pelts which are sent to the tanner must be treated in some way to prevent their decomposition. This is usually done by salting or drying them. The tanner does not find the dried pelts so easy to work as those which have been salted. Pelts from a meat packing plant generally arrive at the tannery in a fresh condition and are kept under refrigeration until tanning begins. Such pelts are called *green*.

Tanning is a complicated but interesting process. Pelts are tanned to prevent decomposition and to make them tough and pliable. The main processes involved in tanning a pelt fall into three large groups: (1) preparation for tanning, (2) actual tanning processes, and (3) finishing processes.

Today most leather is produced by either chrome or vegetable tanning, depending upon the use which will be made of it. However, there are numerous other tanning methods. For shoe uppers, gloves, and garments, chrome-tanned leather is generally used. Harness, luggage, shoe soles, upholstery, and craft items are generally made from vegetable-tanned leather. If tooling or carving is to be done in craft work, the leather *must* be vegetable-tanned since chrome-tanned leather will not tool.

Preparation for tanning

No matter what method of tanning is to be used, the numerous steps taken to prepare the pelts are much alike. In brief, they are first soaked in clear water or a weak chemical solution. This soaking removes the dirt, blood, and salt from the pelts and makes them soft and pliable. The soaking time varies with the condition of the pelts. Dried ones naturally require a longer time. Hides are generally split down the back at this time to make them easier to handle. The two pieces are then called sides.

The next step is fleshing. The softened pelts are fed through machines where sharp revolving knives remove all fat and flesh left on the under side. The hair is generally loosened by immersing the pelts in a lime solution for several days. They are then forced through the de-hairing machine where blunt revolving knives remove the hair. The pelts must next be de-limed by washing and rewashing them in clear water. If complete de-liming is desired, they may be placed in a weak acid solution. The pelts are now ready for the actual tanning processes. They are free of flesh and hair, certain chemical changes have taken place, and the pores have been opened up to permit the penetration of the tanning materials.

Actual tanning processes

In *vegetable* tanning, the method used today remains much the same as that used thousands of years ago by the Hebrews. The tanning material generally used is still oak bark. The pelts are hung in tanks containing a solution of water and the tanning extracts from oak bark or other plant materials. The solution is made stronger each day by the addition of more tanning extracts until the pelts are thoroughly penetrated by the solution. They are then removed from the tanks and placed in large vats. A layer of pelts is sprinkled with ground oak bark, covered with another layer of pelts, a layer of bark, etc. The tanning solution is added. Pelts may remain in the vats for as long as six months, depending upon their thickness and the uses to which they will be put as finished leather.

At the end of this treatment, the pelts are ready for the various finishing processes.

In *chrome* tanning, after the pelts have been prepared, they are placed in large metal drums or tanks with water and common salt is added to open up the pores. Then certain chromium salts are mixed in and the pelts tumbled. Within a few hours chrome-tanned leather is produced.

Finishing processes

Like the steps in preparation for tanning, the finishing processes for both vegetable- and chrome-tanned leathers are much alike. Pelts coming from the tanning solutions must be washed and rinsed to remove excess tanning materials, after which they are pressed to smooth them out. They are then ready for the various finishing processes.

Skins may be put through shaving machines to produce a uniform thickness. Since hides are thick, many of them go to the splitting room where they are split into several layers of various thicknesses. The splitting is done on a machine which has a horizontal blade against which the leather is forced by rollers. The machine is so accurate that the splits do not vary 1/500 of an inch. The weight of leather is measured in ounces. One ounce denotes a thickness of 1/64"; therefore, three-ounce leather is 3/64" thick, eight-ounce 1/8" thick, etc. Splitting is done to secure leathers of thicknesses suitable for shoe uppers, upholstery, and craft work. The outside of a pelt is called the *grain* side and the inside the *flesh* side. Splits from the grain side are stronger and better than those from the flesh side. See Fig. 365.

The tanning processes have left the leather dry and hard. Various oils such as fish oil, soaps, and greases must be worked into the leather to make it soft and pliable.

If a colored leather is desired, the pelts are placed in coloring drums and immersed in hot water. A dye solution is added and the drums rotated for a period of time. The dyes most generally used are coal tar dyes. Uniformity of color

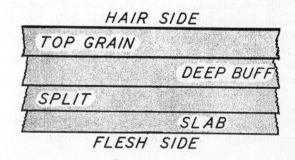

Fig. 365. Method of splitting a hide

may be obtained by rubbing, spraying, or brushing dye upon the surface. Pelts differ greatly in their reactions to dyes.

After the leather has been colored, it may go through a number of other finishing processes which tend to smooth and soften it and make it more flexible. It is then ready for drying. This is done by pasting the leather to special frames or by stretching and fastening it to frames where it dries smooth and free from wrinkles.

If a glazed finish is desired, the leather is rubbed with glass rollers under great pressure. If a high polish is not necessary, it is polished with roller brushes. Suedes are produced by buffing the flesh side to produce the nap or fine pile characteristic of suede.

Many leathers with a very distinctive natural grain such as alligator, lizard, and ostrich are expensive. They may be imitated by embossing their grain upon a less expensive leather such as sheep. These fancy grains are produced by use of an embossing plate under enormous pressure and heat.

The natural grain of leathers is developed by hand graining. This is a skilled operation. It is done by men who use a special cork armboard to apply pressure to the leather which is folded grain-to-grain side. It is rubbed forward, backward, and across; then refolded and rubbed again and again until the desired effect is obtained.

After the finishing processes are completed, the edges of the leather are trimmed and it is sorted for quality and weight. Machines measure the thickness and size of each pelt and these are marked upon it. The skins are rolled into bundles, generally of a dozen skins, and the sides into bundles of three. The leather is then ready to be shipped from the tannery to the many factories and craft houses where it will be put to its final use.

Suggested tool and supply lists

The prices of the tools are not listed since they vary over a period of time. The quality of a tool also determines the price. No quantity amounts are suggested for supplies, the supply list being merely a check list. The amount of supplies will be determined by the time spent and the number of people working. It is suggested that a leathercraft catalog be used to obtain the prices for the tools and supplies in the suggested lists. In this way the total cost of tools and supplies may be determined. Read the information on "Tips on Buying Tools and Supplies."

Minimum tools for a class of 20 students

An individual tool kit is made up of one each of the tools listed.

10 bevel point knives
10 steel squares, 12" x 1" x 7" x 1"
8 tracers
12 No. 471 modelers
3 deerfoot modelers
3 ball-end modelers
6 thonging chisels, four-prong ³⁄₃₂"
1 thonging chisel, four-prong ⅛"
3 thonging chisels, one-prong ³⁄₃₂"
1 thonging chisel, one-prong ⅛"
2 revolving punches, 6-tube
2 eyelet setters
6 hickory or rawhide mallets
1 snap button attaching set

12 cutting boards
12 pieces of marble slab, 1" thick
2 three-foot rules
1 coarse oilstone
2 fine oilstones
24 lacing needles
1 fid
6 scratch awls
1 pr. dividers, 6"
1 edge beveler
1 common edge tool, No. 5
1 edge creaser, No. 1
1 edge creaser, No. 4
2 space markers, 5 and 7 stitches
1 pkg. glover's needles, No. 0-4
6 small paint brushes

Tools for carving
2 nonadjustable swivel knives, junior size
2 nonadjustable swivel knives
4 adjustable swivel knives
8 jeweler's rouge boards

The following stamp numbers refer to both Osborne and Craftool stamps. The letter with a number refers to the Osborne stamps. Consult your craft catalogs for additional stamp numbers and impressions. Also see Fig. 145.

6 No. 101 or A2 background tools
6 No. 203 or C1 smooth bevelers
6 No. 206 or D4 smooth shaders
4 No. 708 or F13 veiners

Suggested additional helpful tools for a class of 20 students

2 cement jars
2 head knives
1 draw gauge
2 stipplers
1 pr. leather shears
6 sewing hafts
6 harness awls, No. 45
1 pkg. harness needles, No. 0-4
1 pr. lacing pliers
6 striking sticks
1 sewing machine
1 embossing wheel and carriage
6 embossing wheels, assorted
2 Segma snap tools, 2 sizes

6 round drive punches, No. 0, 2, 4, 6, 8, 10
3 oblong drive punches, ½", ¾", 1"
1 rampart gouger
1 shoe hammer
1 patent leather compasses
1 lock stitch sewing awl
1 Skife
1 stitching punch
2 English-point punches, ¾", 1"
1 combination punch
1 stitching horse
4 jaw-clamps
1 Vibro-Tool

1 set alphabet stamps, ¾"
1 hand spot tool
2 grommet setting dies, No. 0, 2
4 No. 104 or A4 background tools
4 No. 197 or C3 smooth bevelers
4 No. 702 or C7 fine checked bevelers
2 No. 210 or D6 ribbed horizontal shaders
2 No. 748 or F4 shell tools
4 No. 429 or G8 camouflage tools
6 No. 709 or G4 camouflage tools
1 No. 343 or L7 seeder
2 No. 706 or L2 seeders
2 No. 451 or J2 mule foot

Minimum supply check list

Some supplies may be purchased at local stores and shoe repair shops. If in doubt of the amount of supplies to order, order only a small quantity. After working in leathercraft for some time, you will be able to determine the quantity of supplies needed.

small cellulose sponges

tracing paper

masking or cellophane tape

soft cloths

waxed paper

rubber cement

Barge cement

crocus cloth

tooling sheep

tooling calf, 3- to 4-oz.

strap leather, 3- to 4-oz.

strap leather, 6- to 7-oz.

strap leather, 8- to 9-oz.

lace, 3⁄32″

leather dyes

leather lacquer

thread, cotton, No. C, D

snap fasteners

key case frames

rapid rivets

sheep's wool

oxalic acid crystals

eyelets

bag strap buckles, ½″

Suggested additional supplies

With these supplies, a well-rounded leathercraft program can be conducted.

calf, 1½- to 2-oz.

embossed calf

tooling steerhide

hair calf

alligator

Morocco goat

cowhide splits

lace, ⅛″

lace, Florentine

edge enamels

sole and heel dressing

neutral edge and casing compound

saddle soap

antique finishes

neatsfoot oil compound

castor oil, pure

Lexol

beeswax

nylon thread, No. C, E

flax thread

Segma snaps

grommets

split rivets

copper rivets

ornamental spots

zippers

buckles

dee rings

rectangular loops

nickel staples, for belt loops

looseleaf binder metals

portfolio catches

bag locks

Selected reference list

This list of books is given as a source of special requirements. It is not intended as a complete listing of all books available for leathercraft. Your leathercraft supply company will have most of these books in stock.

Aller, Doris, *Leathercraft Book.* Menlo Park, California: Lane Publishing Company, 1952.
    (For belt, purse, and shoe patterns)
Baird, F. O., *Leather Secrets.* Manitou Springs, Colorado: by F. O. Baird, Publisher, 1951.
    (For a great variety of carving designs and patterns)
Dean, John W., *Leathercraft Techniques and Designs.* Bloomington, Illinois: McKnight & McKnight Publishing Company, 1949.
    (For many styles of lacing stitches)
Grant, Bruce, *Leather Braiding.* Cambridge, Maryland: Cornell Maritime Press, 1950.
    (For many styles of leather braiding)
Griffin, Ken, *The Art of Leather Carving.* Los Angeles: The Craftool Company.
    (For carving designs and patterns)
Griffin, Ken, *Scrap Book.* Los Angeles: Craftool Company, 1952.
    (For carving designs and patterns)
Griswold, Lester, *Handicraft—Simplified Procedure and Projects.* Colorado Springs, Colorado: Lester Griswold, Publisher, 1951.
    (For leather and all other crafts)
Groneman, Chris H., *Leather Tooling and Carving.* Scranton, Pennsylvania: International Textbook Company, 1950.
    (For gun holster patterns)
Stohlman, Al, *Figure Carving.* Los Angeles: Craftool Company, 1953.
    (For figure carving and coloring)
Woolf, Natalie, *Glovemaking for Beginners.* Bloomington, Illinois: McKnight & McKnight Publishing Company, 1951.
    (For many styles of glove patterns)

Index